DID ATLANTIS EXIST
A New Look At Pre-History

Ernest R. Rugenstein PhD

DID ATLANTIS EXIST
A New Look At Pre-History

FICTION4ALL

A FICTION4ALL PAPERBACK

© Copyright 2021
Ernest R. Rugenstein PhD

The right of Ernest R. Rugenstein to be identified as author and channel of this work has been asserted by him in accordance with the Copyright, Designs and Patents Act 1988.

All Rights Reserved

No reproduction, copy or transmission of the publication may be made without written permission.

No paragraph of this publication may be reproduced, copied or transmitted save with the written permission of the publisher, or in accordance with the provisions of the Copyright Act 1956 (as amended).

Any person who does any unauthorised act in relation to this publication may be liable to criminal prosecution and civil claims for damages.

ISBN: 978-1-78695-730-6

This Edition
Published 2022
Fiction4All
www.fiction4all.com

Preface

Ever since I was young, I heard about this mythical place called Atlantis. A great city that met its doom and fell beneath the ocean. Of course, as I grew older there were numerous stories. I read Edgar Casey and his many prophecies, Erich von Dänikin and the *Chariots of the Gods* and the UFO magazines of the 1960's which always talked about aliens, the Philadelphia Experiment, and Atlantis. Most of the magazines talked about how Atlantis was connected to the Bimini Road and the Bermuda Triangle.

Atlantis was always called a magical place. A location where most "rational people" knew was just a myth and those of the "New Age" faith believed Atlantis to be the origin of perfection and the lost religious direction of the world. Atlantis was described by some as the picture of heaven in the Bible to an advanced technological giant like something out of *Stargate Atlantis*.[1]

During my later student career in academia I focused on history, religion and culture, eventually earning a PhD in Cultural History. The one thing a doctorate instills in you is to ask questions.

After teaching World History, Western Civilization, Native American History along with various other history and sociology courses, it seemed that for all the time humans had been on the planet, why all the development in just the last 6000 years.

Part of my Cultural History pursuits included experience as an archaeologist. Beginning in 2017 I initiated a dig in the Adirondacks and wanted to know more about the geology in the area of the dig. Choosing to "bone-up" on my geology I turned to a number of people online. One of the people I came across was Nick Zenter and was fascinated by his description of great floods in the Northwest. Three others I became acquainted through my research were Charles C. Mann, Graham Hancock and Randal Carlson, who changed my perspective on ancient history. Other people that revised my outlook on history were John Anthony West and Robert Schoch with their work on the water erosion of the Sphinx. Alongside these scholars there were the investigations of Natalis Rosen and George S. Alexander and their film *Visiting Atlantis*. Then in 2018, there was the discovery of a meteorite crater in Greenland which supported some of the conclusions of Zenter and Carlson. At that point I knew I had to rethink history.

This book comes about from a course I taught on *Rethinking Pre-history* and the possibility of Atlantis existing. It's a compilation of information from previous mentioned, investigations and research. I consider this work a tertiary source and as such a compilation of information from the sources already mentioned with my thoughts interspersed.

What this book doesn't examine is UFO's. aliens, or the supernatural. If you are looking for that, this book isn't for you. However, if you are interested in a review of human development and the possibility of an historic Atlantis, the prospect of it being a real place then you might want to peruse this writing and perhaps rethink your concept of the past.

Ernest R. Rugenstein, PhD
Cultural History

Table of Contents

Preface

Introduction

Relative Sources Utilized

Chapter 1
Genus Homo to Early Homo Sapiens

Chapter 2
The Cultures of the Mesolithic & Neolithic Ages

Chapter 3
The Younger Dryas Cataclysmic Event and the End of Prior Civilizations?

Chapter 4
Atlantis: What would it have been like?

Appendix 1
Plato's Atlantis Writings 360 BCE

Appendix 2
Maps & Enlarged Photos

Appendix 3
Further Resource Material

End Notes

Introduction

When most people think of history they think of high school and the old name /date /place sort of history. For the most part it was little more than political hero worship regardless as to where you live. What most don't realize is that history is dynamic. New facts, new archaeological finds, reexamination of archives and interpretation of these finds are occurring all the time changing the way we look at the past which updates the story of time.

Occasionally, instead of being welcomed and celebrated this new information is scorned and discredited because of professional snobbism or religious beliefs. This book embraces a new look at pre-history incorporating recent discoveries and interpretations concerning the world prior to 12,000 years ago.

Chapter1 examines recent discoveries of the Genus Homo from Homo Erectus to Homo Sapien Sapiens (modern humans). The chapter reviews the most successful of the Genus Homo, Homo Erectus to the period 45,000 years ago when Homo Sapien Neanderthalus, Homo Sapien Denisovan and Homo Sapien Sapiens walked the earth together.

Chapter 2 reviews the cultures of the Mesolithic and Neolithic societies after the younger dryas event approximately 12,000 years ago. Chapter 3 investigates what has become known as the younger dryas cataclysmic event and the possibilities of civilizations being extinguished.

Chapter 4 looks at Atlantis, what it would have been like and what happened to it. Intuitively, the demise of Atlantis is subjective, however, this chapter's propositions draw on recent scientific scholarship and new historical and archaeological findings. The chapter then extrapolates findings from younger Mesopotamian civilizations in conjunction with new historical and archaeological findings to give us sense of Atlantis' culture. Additionally, Chapter 4 examines the lack of evidence at the Richat Structure proposing what happened to the structures and the Atlantan's extraordinary technologies.

There are three appendices. These include the Appendix 1 containing a translation of the writings of Plato, Appendix 2 contains maps and enlarged photos used in the book, and Appendix 3 containing additional critical and useful resources.

Relevant Sources Utilized

In creating this tertiary source various resources were investigated with some contributing in a direct way through paraphrasing or quoting. Typically, these would be included in a bibliography or works cited page at the end and after endnotes.

However, many times these sources are neglected and not researched by the casual reader. Therefore, I've placed them here for those who may wish to review them before reading this book.

Appendix 3, *Further Resource Material*, are sources not directly used in this book but were general background information. They are important and stimulating resources that should be reviewed.

Dalley, Stephanie, *Myths from Mesopotamia*, (Oxford: Oxford University Press), 1989.

deMenocal, Peter B. & Jessica E. Tierney. *Green Sahara: African Humid Periods Paced by Earth's Orbital Changes*, (Cambridge, MA: Nature Education) https://www.nature.com/scitable/knowledge/library/green-sahara-african-humid-periods-paced-by-82884405/.

Gems, Gerald R., *The Athletic Crusade: Sport and American Imperialism* (Lincoln: University of Nebraska Press), 2006.

Howard, Brian Clark. *City-size impact crater found under Greenland Ice. National Geographic* ttps://www.nationalgeographic.com/science/2018/11/impact-crater-found-under-hiawatha-glacier-greenland-ice/.

Muratori, *Chronicon Estense in Rerum Italicarum Scriptores*, 15, III. pp. 159-164 as cited by Phillip Ziegler, *The Black Death,* (New York: Harper Collins) 1969.

NOAA: National Centers for Environmental Information. *Perspectives Abrupt Climate Change: The Younger* Dryas, Department of Commerce: US Government, https://www.ncdc.noaa.gov/abrupt-climate-change/The%20Younger%20Dryas.

NS Gill, *Atlantis as It Was Told in Plato's Socratic Dialogues*, Thoughtco, https://www.thoughtco.com/platos-atlantis-from-the-timaeus-119667, October 5, 2018.

Old Testament (Torah) Genesis 6:9-9:17

Orkneyjar - The Heritage of the Orkney Islands, http://www.orkneyjar.com

Sharing Resources, A Community Learning Center, HawaiiHistory.org, Info Graik Inc., 2020.

Chapter 1
Genus Homo to Early Homo Sapiens

As we begin to look at pre-history it's important to get a handle on time designations that are commonly used in typical dating systems. This might seem a bit pedantic but as I tell my students it's important to have a good base of understanding to build on.

Most are familiar with the "B.C." & "A.D." designation. "B.C." stands for the English phrase "before Christ," whereas "A.D." stands for the Latin phrase: anno domini (in the year of the Lord) starting the year Jesus was "born." So, what we find is that there is no "0 BC" or "AD 0." The time designation goes from 1 BC to AD 1. The problem with these designations is that there was a great deal of assumptions made and a lack of exact data. Many Biblical scholars now agree that "Jesus" was born between 6 BC and AD 4. Therefore, a more modern designation came into effect, "BCE" (Before the Common Era) used in modern text instead of "B.C." and "CE" (Common Era) is used instead of "A.D." Again, there is no "0 BCE" or "CE 0" with the classification going from "1 BCE" to "CE 1."

There are a number of other designations that pop-up when looking at ancient history. These include: kya – Thousands of Years Ago, mya – Millions of Years Ago, and bya – Billions of Years Ago. Other designations encountered when viewing dates, RcyBp - *Radiocarbon Years Before Present* is one of these. The term "BP" (*Before Present*) uses the year CE 1950 as "Present" which was the year radiocarbon calibration curves were being established.

Another aspect that needs to be engaged are the relative time periods on Earth. The *Flintstones* cartoon series although funny and creative were not documentaries. Humans and dinosaurs never walked the earth together, not once. What we typically think of dinosaurs went extinct about 65 mya. The closest a bipedal hominid came to a living dinosaur was Australopithecus an extinct hominid that lived between 3.9 and 2.9 mya in Africa. Not a modern human (Homo sapien sapien) but a hominid. In fact, when talking about change, the earth itself had changed over the time period between dinosaurs and humans.

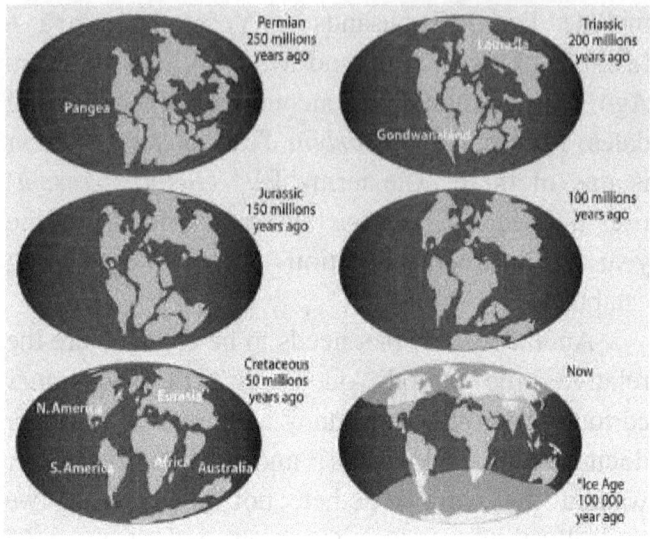

Even our perception of who is a human is now challenged with current scholarship. Homo sapiens came in different "flavors" such as Neanderthals, Sapiens and Denisovans all of which walked the earth together and interbred until 40 kya. In fact, we know from DNA mapping that Europeans have both Sapien and Neanderthal DNA (up to 2 %) whereas Melanesian have Sapien and Denisovans DNA (up to to 5%).

When considering pre-history, the question comes up what exactly do, we mean by history? To many scholars history is a product of written documents and/or archaeological excavations. Oral histories are usable if verified through archaeological finds or extrapolated data. Otherwise they are considered myths, fables, or folktales. The exception of course is, when taking firsthand accounts of a person's life or what they have witnessed.

As time goes on some of these so-called myths, fables, or folktales take on new meanings and openings for inquiry such as a great flood has taken on a new light. These myths, fables, or folktales become the basis of new peer-reviewed, possibly unorthodox, investigation.

Anthropologist and cultural historians remind us that the concept of writing can take a number of different forms. Writing could be knots tied on "strings" as with the Inca's quipu (knot-recording)[2], to Wampum used by a number of Native American Nations to pictographs or symbols still in use worldwide. Finally, it's essential that history concerns anthropological studies otherwise of course, it would be considered natural history. Nevertheless, as we explore the concept of pre-history there is an interesting melding of human history & natural history.

Hominoids & Hominids

An aspect of pre-history needed to be grasped is the evolution of humanity. Some feel humans were created by divine aspirations, however when looking through the lens of science we find another understanding. What's wonderful about science is that in its purist form, science isn't dogmatic and can say, "with new evidence our previous conclusions were wrong."

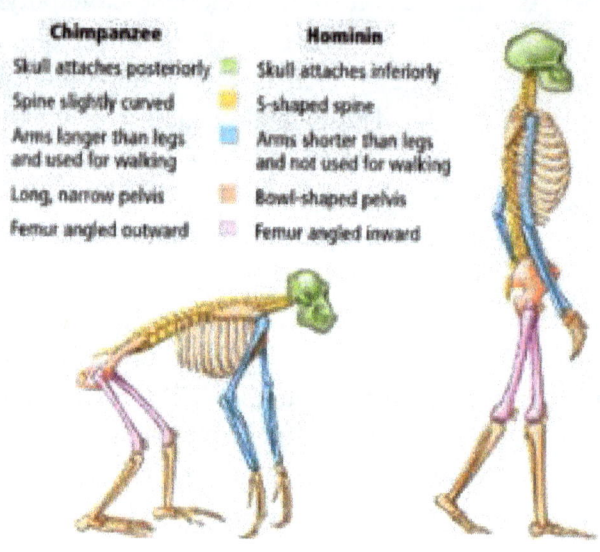

As we move forward it is important to understand where hominoids and hominids fit into the evolution of humans. Hominoids include all the apes, gibbons, gorillas, chimps, orangutans and humans. When we look at humans' closer relatives, we find the hominids.

Hominids include all modern and extinct great apes. This means that chimps, gibbons, gorillas, orangutans, etc. aren't included. Basically, any of early human species that is more closely related to humans than chimpanzees, including modern humans themselves are under the sub-heading hominids.

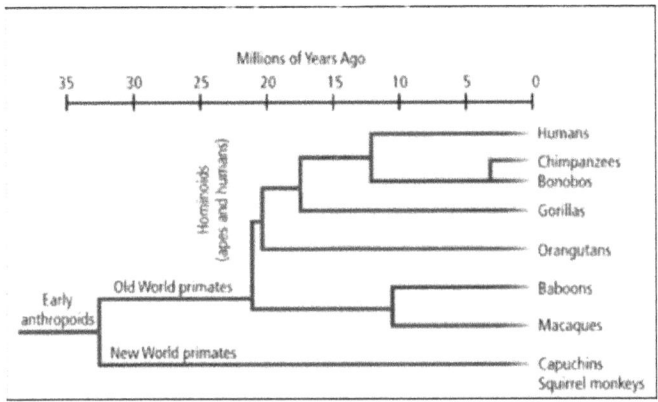

Hominoids and Hominids were able to adapt the environment to themselves and from anthropological studies the two groups were able to use tools and a primitive language. Animals on the other hand had to deal with the environment as they found it.

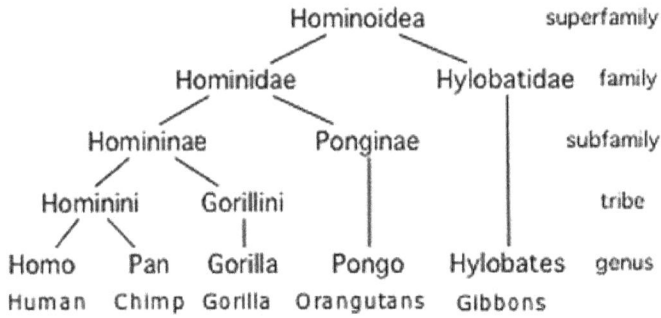

Complex cooperative social structures are found with hominoids and hominids. Animals have complex social structures; however, they tend to be more instinctual.

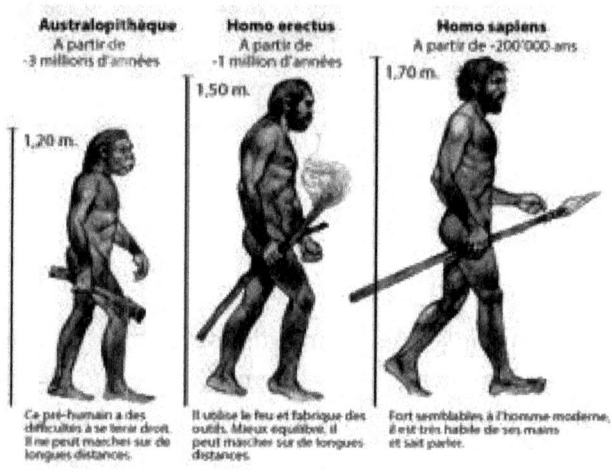

Early Hominids

One of the earliest discovered hominids was an Australopithecus that was given the name "Lucy." The skeleton was discovered and excavated north of Addis Ababa in Ethiopia. With 40% of skeleton (AL-288-1) found it was speculated that "she" had an overall height of between 137 – 138 centimeters (approximately 4 ½ feet), a weight of about 25 Kg. (55 lbs.) and importantly bipedal.

The Australopithecus brain was found to be approximately 500 cc (30½ in^3), whereas a modern human brain is 1400 cc (85 in^3). Along with bipedalism another aspect of "Lucy" that was important was her all-important opposable digit.

Limited speech may have been possible however there is conjecture about the variety of sounds she could have made. Anybody who has been around a 9-month-old baby, however, realizes that a small number of sounds can create a great deal of communication.[3]

"Lucy's" estimated date of death was roughly 3.5 mya, 60 million-years after the extinction of the dinosaurs, again no human interaction with dinosaurs.

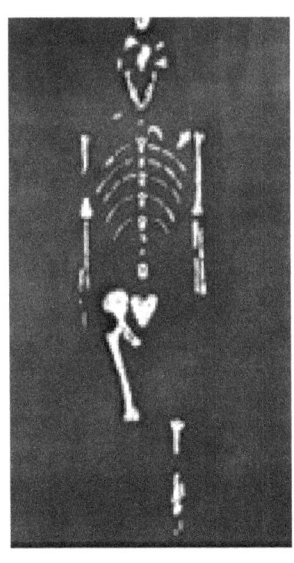

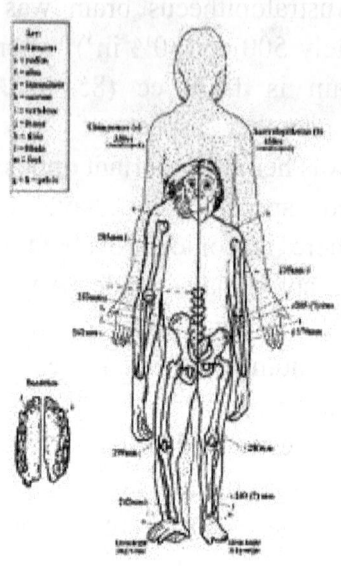

Later Hominids

Hominidae (order Primates) and the genus Homo include a number of species and sub-species that are characterized by a relatively large cranial capacity, limb structure adapted to standing erect and bipedal walking. They also have opposable thumbs, dexterous hands with precision grips, and able to make standardized precision tools with the skill of using one tool to make another. These later Hominids additionally could create artwork and had concern for the dead.

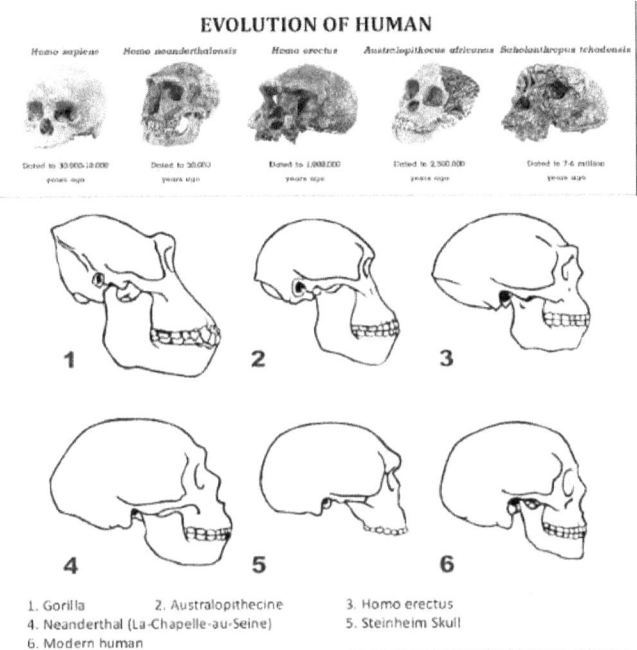

1. Gorilla
2. Australopithecine
3. Homo erectus
4. Neanderthal (La-Chapelle-au-Seine)
5. Steinheim Skull
6. Modern human

There have been a number of theories as to why the members of the Genus Homo walk upright and are bipedal. Typically, the thinking centers around the idea that our predecessors partly stood because they lived on the Savannah of Africa; standing gave them the ability to see over tall grasslands, with more agility for hunting and defense.

A more recent theory deals with water and points to evidence that our genus brothers and sisters lived near or on the shore of waterways, lakes and of course the ocean. Because of using water for transportation, and gathering food, genus homo hominids adapted bipedal movement to move into deeper water. Further there is evidence that the females gave birth in water as been practiced in recent years.

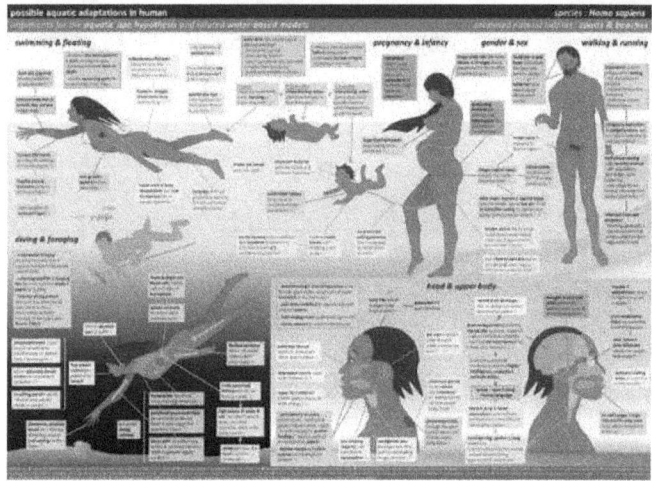

A later Hominids, Homo Erectus (Homo Ergaster), was one of the most successful of the Genus Homo. Homo Erectus ("upright man") had a two-million-year presence as well as a large range of existence from Africa to across Eurasia. (1.8 mya to possibly 100 kya)

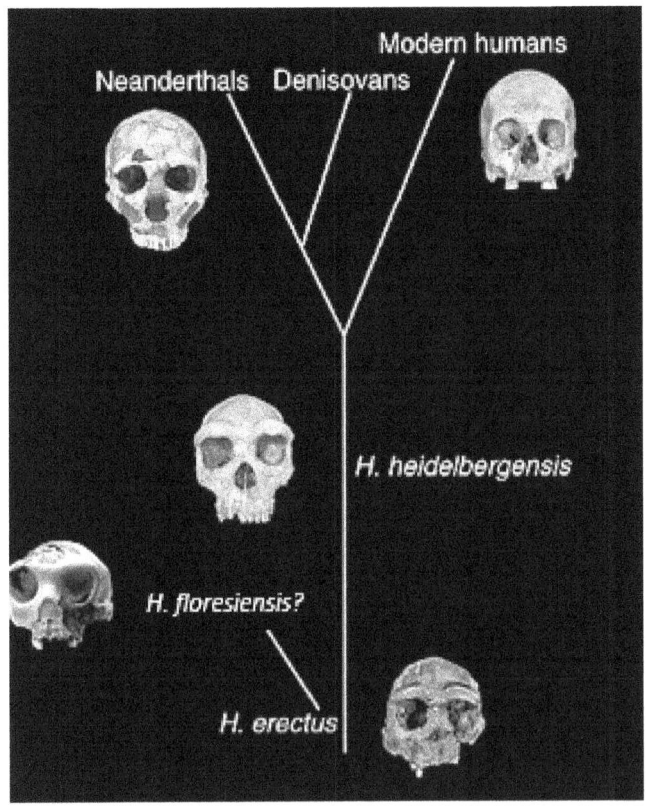

Differences between H. Erectus and Australopithecus included the lack of skeletal features for climbing, and the fact the H. Erectus had appendages in the same proportions as modern humans.

Australopithecus' had a height of about 1 meter tall where H. Erectus had varying height from 1.6 meters to 1.8 meters (6 feet). H. Erectus' diet included meat as well as plant and tuber material.

There is further evidence that they cooked their meat and created complex tools much as later Genus Homo did. Not only did H. Erectus have improved tool use they could easily control fire and probably had a language.

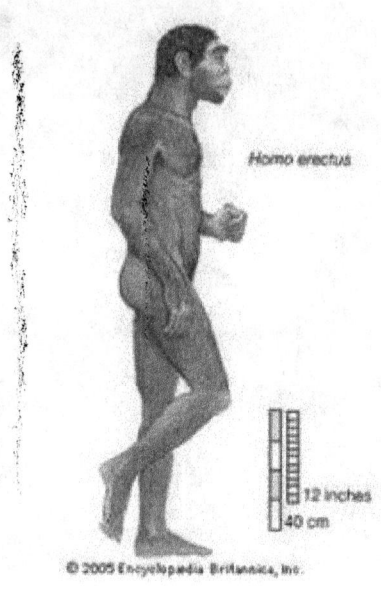

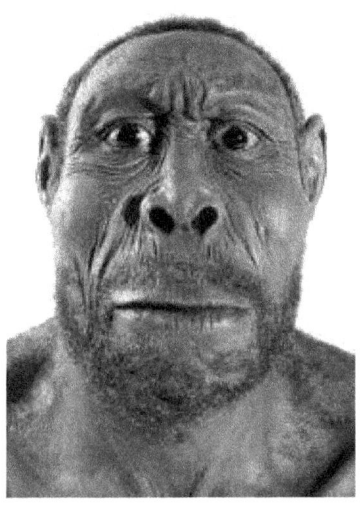

Homo Floresiensis, generally, considered to be descended from H. Erectus and is separate from Homo Sapiens. They were found on the Island of Flores in Indonesia with evidence showing that they existed from approximately 95 kya until 17 kya. They tended to be 1.06 meters tall (3½ feet) with body proportions to that of modern humans. Currently it is thought that H. Floresiensis achieved its size proportions through evolutionary dwarfism. Evolutionary dwarfism is common in other animal species and is typically caused by limited resources and constriction of hunting-gathering range as on an island.

Homo Heidelbergensis, is an evolved form of H. Erectus which existed between 600 kya to 200 kya in Europe, Asia, and Africa. It is the link between H. Erectus and later H. Sapiens. H. Heidelbergensis had similar facial features as H. Erectus but had a larger brain cavity and smaller teeth and jaw line such as H. Sapiens.

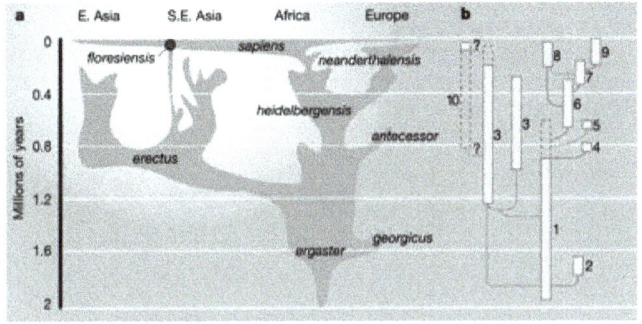

Homo Sapiens descended from H. Heidelbergensis approximately 500 kya and includes the Homo Sapien subspecies of Neanderthalensis, Denisovans, and Sapiens.

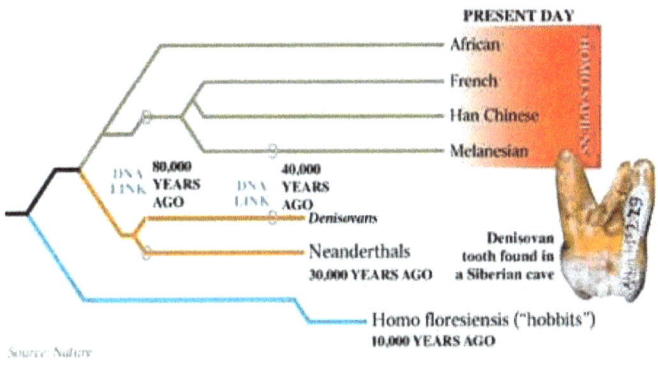

The migrations of H. Erectus and H. Sapiens were worldwide raging all of Africa, Eurasia, South East Asian Islands, and Australia. These treks persisted for 1000's of years and guided by need.

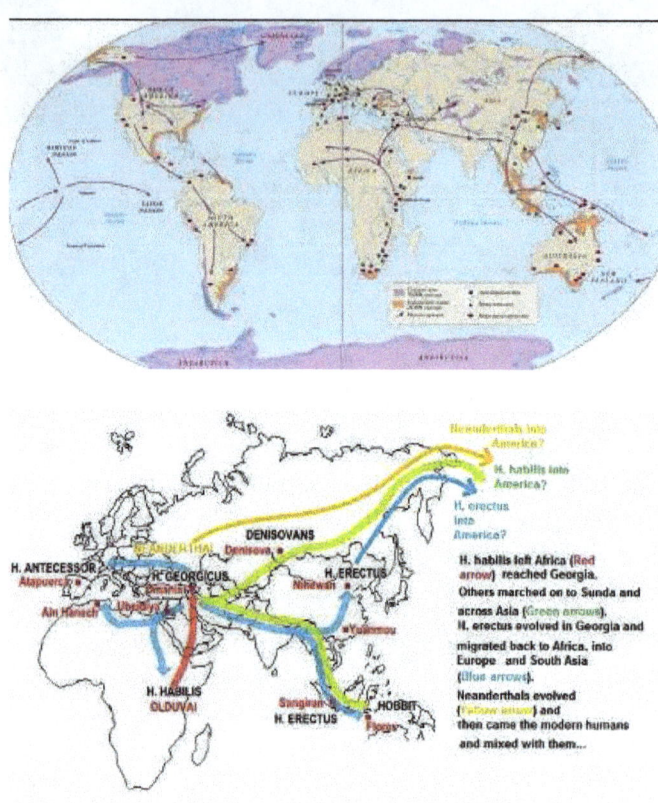

Current scholarship informs us there were three Homo Sapiens species roaming the earth up to 35 kya. These included, Homo Sapien Sapien, Homo Sapien Neanderthalensis, and Homo Sapien Denisovan.

Homo Sapien Neanderthalensis:

Homo Sapien Neanderthalensis was first discovered in the Neander valley, of western

Germany in 1856. Additional specimens were found in Europe, Africa, and East Asia. There is significant evidence they were spiritual and conducted ritual burials. Additionally, it's realized that they had artwork (cave paintings & inscribed bone and rock art), crafted musical instruments and interbred with Sapiens and Denisovans.

Neanderthalensis tended to be light skin, had a large vocabulary and via DNA sequencing, shows red hair was common. They roamed the earth between 300 kya – 40 kya.[4]

[Below: Skeleton comparison of Neanderthals (left) & Sapiens (right)]

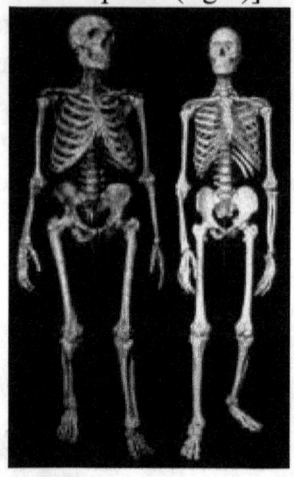

Homo Sapien Denisovan:

Homo Sapien Denisovans were first discovered in the Denisovan Cave in a remote Siberian valley of the Altai mountains. They existed between 300 kya to approximately 50 kya and were coeval with Sapiens and Neanderthalensis.

Current scholarship infers that H.S. Denisovans originated from a group of H.S. Neanderthalensis that were isolated in Asia and developed unique characteristics. Extrapolating from Neanderthalensis it is posited that Denisovans lived in small extended family groups and tended to be hunter-gathers.[5]

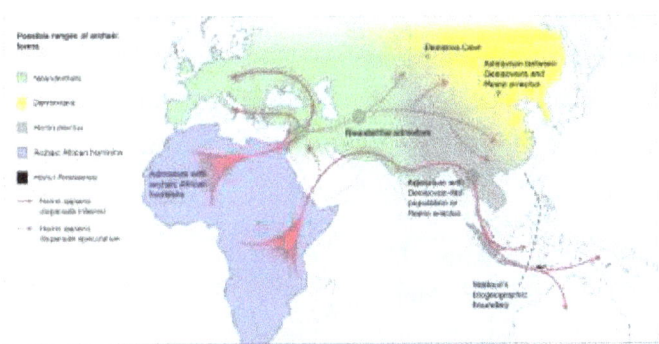

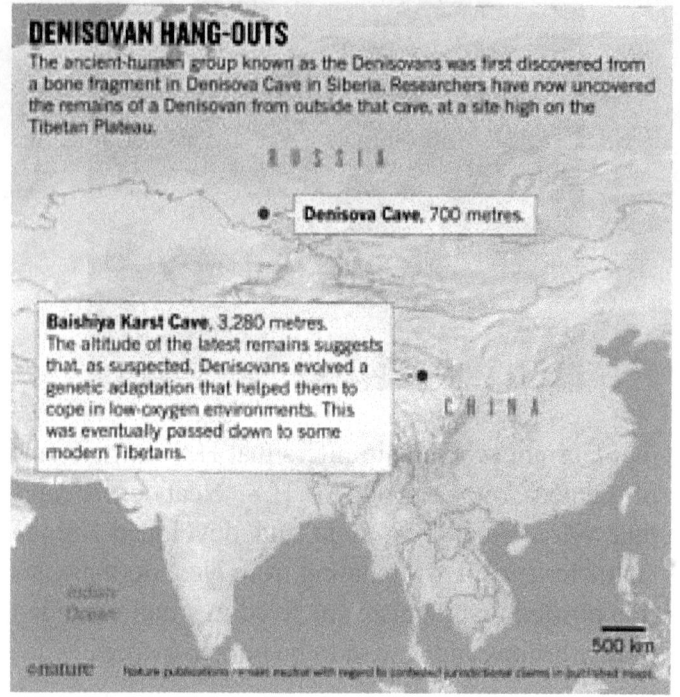

Homo Sapien Sapiens:

The current designation of modern humans include:
    Familia: *Hominidae*
    Subfamilia: *Homininae*
    Tribes: *Hominine*
    Subtribes: *Hominina*
    Genus: *Homo*
    Species: *Homo sapiens*
    Subspecies: *Sapien*

Contemporary research informs us that Homo Sapien Sapiens (modern humans) originated in Africa 300 kya.

Known in the past as the Cro-Magnon peoples of Ice-Age Europe, they are the early Paleolithic humans of Eurasia. They were physically the same as modern humans and had a great capacity for speech. At present they are viewed as having an increase in the variety of tools used and archaeological evidence points to having adornments, and decorative furniture. Further, it appears that they were cultic with the finding of religious "Venus" figurines and the abundant evidence of cave paintings and engraved stone and bone artwork.[6]

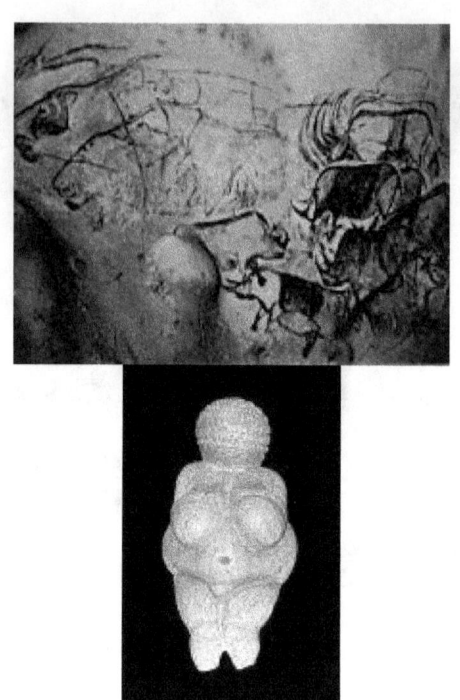

It is essential to take a closer look at the various eras when humans existed. Although the common eras generally written about are the Paleolithic Era, Mesolithic Era, Neolithic Era, Chalcolithic Era, Bronze Age, and the Iron Age, the analysis of this book will deal with only the first three (Paleolithic Era, Mesolithic Era, & Neolithic Era).

Homo Eras:

The Paleolithic Era (old stone age) lasted from 2.6 mya to about 10 kya. Current anthropology and history inform us that during this period of about 2

½ million years humans were just hunter-gatherers. Moreover, except for the last 40,000 years, we had two other Homo Sapien groups on the planet. We will explore this era in greater detail in a later chapter.

The Mesolithic Era (middle stone age) began about 12 kya BCE and lasted until about 7000 BCE. This is an era populated only with modern humans and was the beginning of new tool design, living conditions and hunting techniques. It was a time of humans beginning to settle down.

The Neolithic Era (new stone age) lasted from around 9,000 BCE to about 3,000 BCE. It was a time of people becoming settled farmers with houses, domesticated animals and farm fields.

Remember these eras do not begin and end at a particular date and changes took place over hundreds to thousands of years. In some case, there were those populations that never transited from hunter-gatherers to farmers. They lived in areas that were naturally fruitful and hunting/fishing was easy. They simply didn't need to develop new techniques.

With new archaeological excavations, finding of new data concerning geological alterations, review and interpretation archival records, DNA testing of Native populations, and the loss of archaeology over the increase of ocean depths may skew these time eras and their interpretation of documents, data and dates.

Paleolithic Era ("Old Stone Age")
2.6 mya to about 10 kya:

Evidence for this era comes from a plethora of archaeological excavations and the extrapolation from contemporary hunter-gatherer societies.

Current accepted archaeological/ historical findings state the paleolithic people led a nomadic existence. It is assumed that this situation would preclude any sort of advanced modern civilization. It's felt during this time period groups would consist of extended family groups of about 50 to 100 individuals. The division of Labor would have been divided along gender lines, although not exclusively, for the majority of the population.

Homo Sapien paleolithic culture, being nomadic, did not lend it to land accumulation for farming or mining. The real determinant of status could have been through respect of age, heredity, hunting skills, possibly from fertility or charisma or it might have just been the "biggest-baddest-guy."

From extrapolation it is accepted there was gender equality related to food production generally (not exclusively) with men providing meat from hunting and women providing eatable plants/tubers.

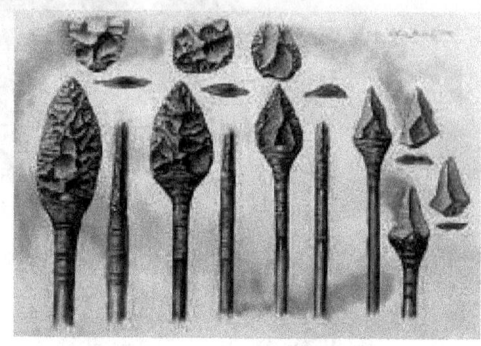

Both endeavors require planning and communication. Hunting requires organization with the possibility of developing specialized weaponry, using animal-skin disguises and stampeding tactics. Gathering plants requires knowledge of what plants are edible, how to harvest and cook them, and which ones can be used medicinally.

I want to reiterate that until 100 kyaBp there were multiple members of Genus Homo and until 40 kyaBp there were multiple Homo Sapien species inhabiting the planet.

Chapter 2
The Cultures of the Mesolithic & Neolithic World

Homo Sapien Sapiens (modern humans) are the only human species still existing from 12 kya to the present. This is the time period of the Mesolithic and Neolithic Eras. Most archaeologist and historians generally agree on the various aspects of these eras, even though there may be some conceptual differences. Any disagreement concerns the when, who, and over multi-millenniums, how many times was this process repeated? However, we will review these eras in connection with currently accepted scholarship.

Mesolithic Era ("Middle Stone Age") 12 kya BCE – 7 kya BCE:

The Mesolithic era is characterized by two major factors; families and groups partially settling down, and the use of small, flaked stone tools called microliths and retouched bladelets.

The use of smaller lithic material allows more versatility in use and quick repair. Instead of taking the time to create a large projectile point, which takes accuracy to extract the right flake from a larger piece of chert or flint and then knap it to its final shape. Microliths could be create and the pieces worked and created to be interchangeable.

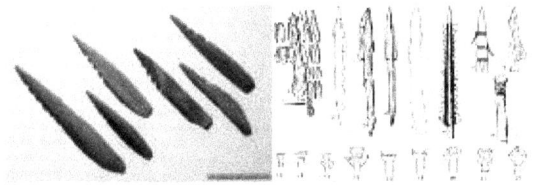

The other aspect of this era is that groups began settling down, herding non-domesticated animals and taking advantage of natural resources. There are a number of examples of this characteristic around the world. The North American Pacific northwest, there is the Chinook society which lived on berries, acorns and salmon. In Japan, the Jomon society relied on fishing and wild buckwheat and in modern Israel and Jordon there was the Natufian which used wild wheat and herded animals.

Mesolithic settlements could have numbered up to 1000 individuals, undoubtedly the size of the community was limited to its natural resources. Many if not most of the Mesolithic settlements have been lost to sea rise.

An example of an area where Mesolithic communities thrived was Dogger Bank. During the Mesolithic Era, this entire area was dry land uniting the British Isles to the rest of the Europe. Because

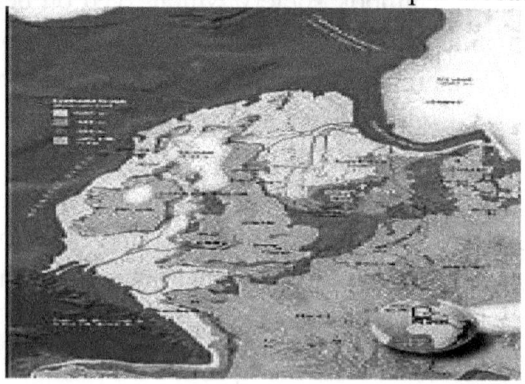

of a number of natural disasters in the Norwegian Sea and the area of Greenland, Dogger Land, known today as Dogger Bank, was partially drenched by a tsunami and eventually flooded by raising sea levels. This situation submerged the Mesolithic populations and drowned settlements and rudimentary farmlands. Today, fishing nets bring up various tools from the era along with butchered animal bones including numerous examples of mammoths.

Neolithic Era ("New Stone Age") 9 kya BCE - 3 kya BCE:

The Neolithic Era can be categorized by settling of humans into farming communities and the launching of worker specialization. This specialization would find that some made tools, others were potters, or created jewelry or art. There may have been those who built buildings or repaired houses and roofs.

Evidence points to farming beginning spontaneously in many parts of the world as opposed to the process of spreading bronze technology from a central area.

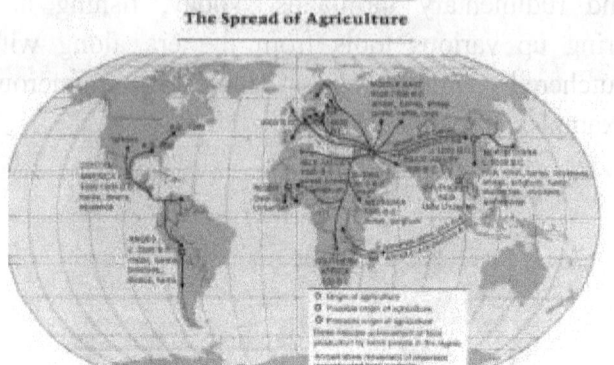

The Spread of Agriculture

Scholars believe that part of the development of farming was the discovery of edible plants growing in midden and "night soil." Many seeds and nuts are not digestible by humans and pass through the digestive track. As for the midden, it would be noticed that discarded seeds and other plant material would grow and produce more "fruit." This growing would eventually be systemized into the type of farming we think of in the Early Middle Ages with the plow developed around 11 kya. With some advancements farming remained essentially the same until the 1600's. We must "tip-our-hat" to the Neolithic farmers and their ability to hybridize grains, fruits, and vegetables similar to what we find on our tables today as portrayed by current scholarship.

The Neolithic Era was one of change and yet people had all the same wants and desires that we have today. Their living conditions would not be that different in many parts of the modern world. In central Europe during this era people lived in homes with thatched roofs including windows and doors.

There are a number of different aspects of this era that should be explored including culture & how each culture was unique in different areas, as in tool production, shelter, and the expansion of agriculture.

Cultural changes: Cultural changes come in a number of ways from art to shelters to even tool production. An example of this is the difference between stone tool production of the Paleolithic period and the Mesolithic/Neolithic. The Paleolithic period used rougher tool production and the tools remained as chipped. The Mesolithic period and even more in the Neolithic period tools were finished, in some cases, polished. Refined style in the use of raw materials for projectiles is observed during this time. Such as, microlithic points being manufactured instead of the larger one-piece projectile points.

It's also the beginning of trade and textile manufacturing. Flax fibers have been found at archaeological digs dating back 36 kya. The fibers could be dyed and used to make linen clothing. As today, styles would be dictated by environmental needs and local/tribal culture preferences.

Cultural changes also bring on specialization of labor. As farming became more efficient and produced more food it allowed others to expand their expertise in other fields such as pottery making (without a wheel), house building, roof repair, and even mining especially if chert or flint were in the area.

Population increases and migration brought about cultural interactions. This produced trade along with interrelated relationships between populaces. These interrelated relationships could also mean war if the Tollense Valley battlefield is any example. Up to 4000 people, some on horseback, fought and died in a battle during the 13th Century BCE in Northern Germany.

One example of cultural differences is the construction of pottery and how it is decorated. The different styles can give a clue as to where it was made in Neolithic Europe.

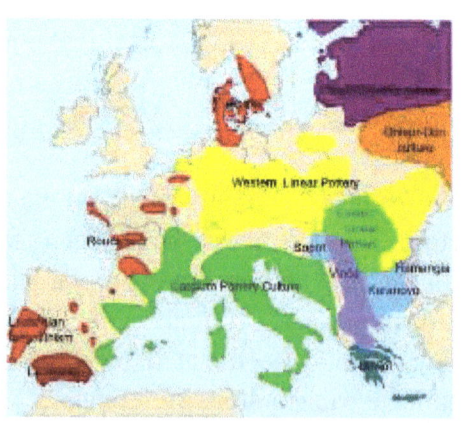

The best illustration of the differences in culture is in the decoration of pottery. Pots, which were hand crafted without a wheel, were painted in southeastern Europe, southern Italy, and Sicily. In other areas they were adorned with incised, impressed, or stamped patterns of various designs.

Some designs were skeuomorphic enhancing the pot's similarity to vessels of basketry, skin, or other material. In central Europe and the Ukraine and in the Balkans, spirals and meanders were the favorite motifs on pottery.

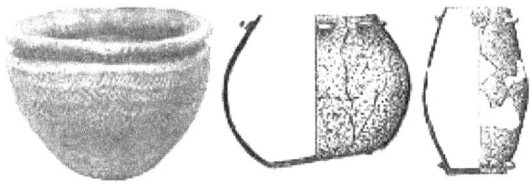

Farming in Europe during the Neolithic period developed along its own line in four different ecological areas. These areas include the Mediterranean area of evergreen forest and winter rains, the Temperate area which is north of the Pyrenees, the Alps, and the Balkans, containing deciduous forest and evenly distributed annual rainfall.

Another area was the Circumpolar taiga which was still farther north of the Temperate area and contained coniferous forest. This was the only area to remain free of agriculture and stock breeding. To the southeast of Europe was the western end of the Eurasian Steppe which was fertile with gently rolling plains. Because of the unique situation of being at relatively the same latitude it allowed similar crops and animals to flourish and be transported along with human migrations.

Farmers living in villages: The Neolithic period brought about settled farmers in farm villages with people living in houses. These houses had windows & doors, furniture and in some cases water tanks to keep fish and other seafood fresh.

The development of farming saw the division of labor along gender lines. Men were tasked with the domestication and/or herding of animals rather than hunting exclusively. Women took on the job of cooking, along with planting and nurturing vegetation rather than foraging. This was the general division of labor; however, women may have taken care of animals, men could have worked in the fields and both men and women could have hunted to supplement the family diet.

Slash-and-and burn techniques were used to prepare the land for farming, nevertheless without having a fallow field in rotation the soil became exhausted. This soil exhaustion promoted periodic migration on regular schedules. Some groups would migrate from one area to another. The cyclic period could have varied from every other planting season to a number of years. When one area was exhausted of resources and getting rid of midden was difficult, they would transport crops and herds from one region to another returning after the initial area was rejuvenated. By 3 kya BCE we find that farming villages started to develop into larger urban areas such as Jericho.

Stone Tools: Stone tools had been used by many hominids and are not limited to Homo Sapiens. H. Erectus used tools for over a million years and H. Sapiens have used tools for their entire existence. It's been found that H.S. Neanderthals and H.S. Sapiens had a greater variety of tools than others of the Genus Homo and although we have little or no evidence it's inferred that H.S. Denisovan did too.

Lamoka Projectile Points 3500-2500 BCE

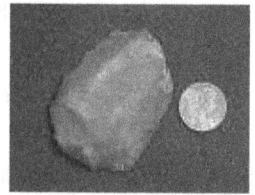

Algonquian Scrapper

Modern humans during the Neolithic period produced high quality tools which had a greater variety of uses.

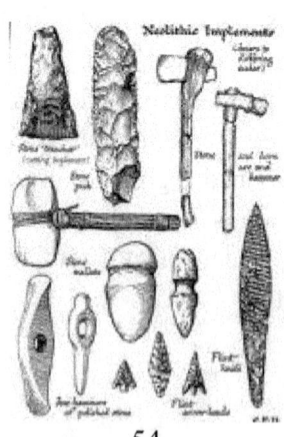

Neolithic peoples used celt, ax, or adz heads edged through the grinding and polishing of fine-grained rock or of flint if the material was available in large nodules. Celts were typically mounted on antler sleeves inserted between the stone head and the wooden handle. Ax heads were simply stuck on to or through straight wooden shafts.

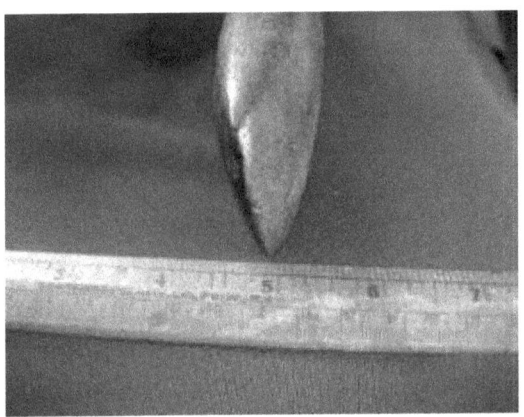

Neolithic Adze Head

Adz heads were characteristically mounted on a knee shaft (a crooked stick). This was also the regular method for attaching ax heads. Ax heads with a hole for the shaft, similar to modern tools, have also been found but they were rarely used. However, along the Danube River some adzes

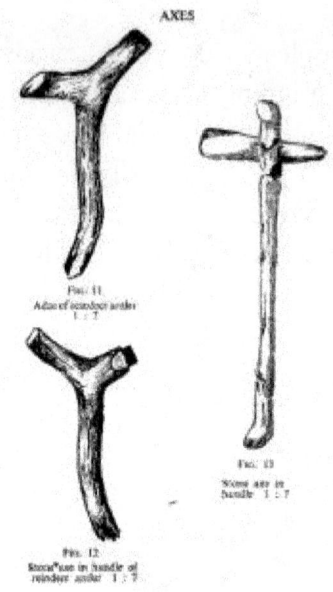

Fig. 11
Adze of reindeer antler
1 : 7

Fig. 12
Stone axe in handle of reindeer antler 1 : 7

Fig. 13
Stone axe in handle 1 : 7

were discovered mounted in this manner. They were manufactured by perforating a hole through the stone by using a tubular borer (a reed or bone with sand as an abrasive). From there the technique was adopted by various secondary Neolithic tribes.

Neolithic Trade & Mining: Neolithic communities were self-sufficient; being able to produce their own food and make tools from local materials. However, some localities had superior chert or flint, where other areas had an abundance of meat, honey, or the ability to provide rare items that were desired such as amber.

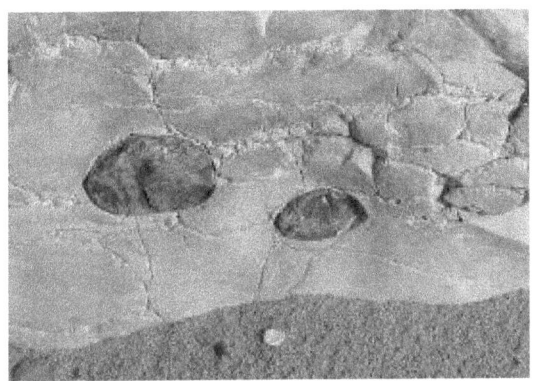
Nodules in chalk. White Park Bay, Ireland

This promoted local and long-distance trade of ornaments and jewelry. The extent of this trade can be seen from jewelry made from Mediterranean shells being found from the Danube Valley to the Balkans. Various raw and rare materials were also traded because of their scarcity in other areas. Raw chert and flint could be traded for rare grains and honey that were plentiful. Another trade item that was desired had high grade clay for making pots. An extremely rare trade item was amber which was seen as divine because of its ability to hold a static charge. This was not a static cultural society but a dynamic one.

Trade was necessary, as it is today, because settlement patterns for farming did not allow every settlement the ability to produce high quality tools and projectile points from local material. Many-times finished, or semi-finished tool forms were traded. Celts, or axes, were manufactured in factories where especially suitable rock outcrops occurred and they were traded over great distances. As in mining today, the Neoliths would find seams and follow the seams of nodules. They would cut mine shafts through solid chalk sometimes to a depth of six meters (20 feet) with antler picks and bone shovels.

Most of the mines were simply pits, however many had galleries branching from them following the seams of big nodules. The Neolithic miners knew the need of supporting the ceiling and left pillars as support. Archaeologists have found skeletons of workers killed by collapses in an adit or a rock fall in a stope. Even though trade was involved the miners should not be seen as specializing in mining exclusively. They would still be farmers tending fields and animals and would-be repairing farm buildings and their own home.

Neolithic Mine

Structures: All of the Genus Homo constructed housing. Caves were used at times and could have been occupied as hunting camps or longer depending on location and environment. Obviously, if the cave was high and dry with good ventilation and close to food and other raw materials needed for survival it would be used. An example of this is Blombos Cave in South Africa which was occupied by both H. S. Neanderthalensis and H. S. Sapien. Evidence points to the cave being occupied between 100 kyaBp - 70 KyaBp and another period between 2 kyaBp - 0.3 kyaBp.

Homo Erectus, the most successful of the Genus Homo constructed structures out of skins stretched over mammoth bones or wood frames. These buildings could be between 26 ft to 49 ft long and 13 ft to 26 ft wide built with stone foundations and at times stone floors. A sophisticated structure for a species which could make a variety of tools 1 mya.

Homo Sapiens used a variety of structures depending on the time period and location. As with H. Erectus, H. Sapiens would have used caves as camps or semi-long-term housing depending on needs and the surrounding environment. During the Paleolithic period, H. Sapiens were hunter gatherers and used temporary housing.

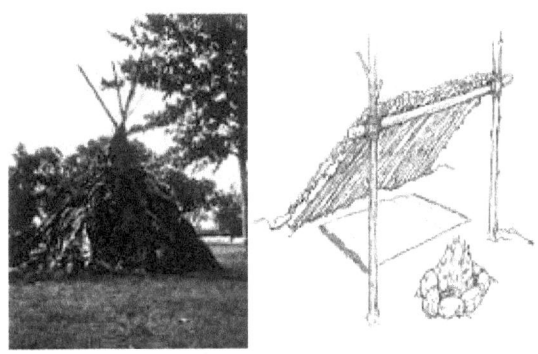

Some groups could have used a "teepee" style structure while at other times skins and poles were used in creating a "lean-to."

If possible and with the right materials a wood and moss-covered structure could have been constructed.

During the Mesolithic and Neolithic periods, we find a change in housing. It becomes more complex and is built for longer period of times. Mesolithic people would migrate periodically to & from the same seasonal grounds.

Neolithic people were settled farmers. Their housing was constructed from various materials found in the area and for the climate.

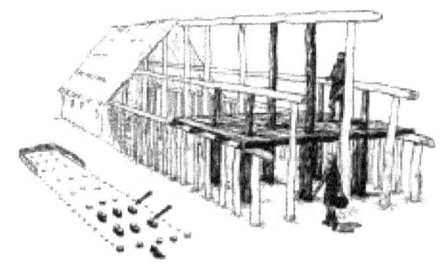

Along the Mediterranean and the Iberian Peninsula houses were built similar to the Middle East. Typically, this would be out of mud brick on a stone foundation. In the temperate zone, wood was used for the construction of gabled houses, stout posts serving to support the ridgepole and the walls of split saplings of wattle and daub.

In Alpine regions along the shores of lakes one or two-roomed houses were built on wooden piles above the shores of the lake or on platforms laid on peat mosses.

In northern Europe, the earliest villages also consisted of two parallel, long communal wooden houses. These were subdivided into 20 or more apartments with a separate door. But here again the communal houses eventually broke up into free-standing one-roomed huts.

Neolithic people also made a number of different earthwork sites. In some locations long-barrows were used. Typically, they were elongated earthen tombs constructed with interior timber or stone chambers containing multiple cremation burials.

Passage Graves were another kind of early Neolithic collective tomb with an internal stone passage covered by a circular earthen mound. Neolithic Causewayed Camps were gathering centers used for feasting and ritual practices. They were surrounded by a number of circles of discontinuous ditches with gaps (causeways) allowing access.

During the later Neolithic period we see the beginnings of the use of henges. Henges were large earthen sites surrounded by circular earthen ditches and banks. The construction also had circular standing timber and stones. As time progressed there was also a change from multiple burials to individual burials in usually smaller earthen mounds or barrows. Remarkably we see similar construction in North America by the Indigenous peoples.

Neolithic Skare Brae: The Neolithic village of Skare Brae is located on southern shore of Sandwick's Bay o' Skaill in Northern Scotland.

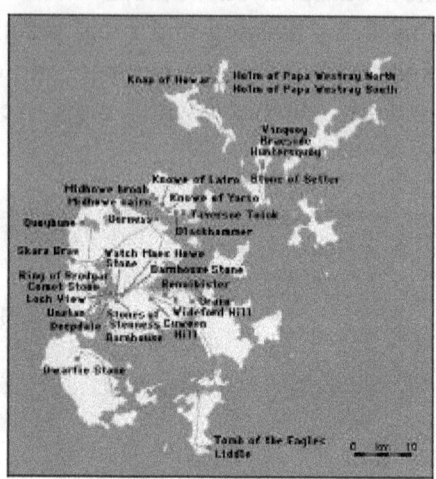

In the winter of 1850, a storm battered Orkney during which the high winds and enormous high tides exposed the interior of a large mound known as Skerrabra. The storm exposed the shape of a series of stone buildings that fascinated the local lord, William Watt of Skaill.

He began excavating the site and by 1868 four ancient houses were excavated; regrettably the site was abandoned, remaining undisturbed until 1925. At that time another storm damaged some of the previously excavated structures.

The buildings that were erected used flagstones layered in the earth as a foundation. The area between the walls was filled with earth and midden for natural insulation. Furniture in the homes was

made of stone and included such things as dressers, cupboards, chairs and even beds.

Hearths indicate the homes were warmed by fire and each home would originally have a roof, perhaps of turf that had some sort of opening to serve as a chimney. Even so, it is thought that the houses, which had no windows, would have been fairly smoky and certainly illuminated from the interior. Each house was constructed along the same design and many have the same sort of furniture and layout of rooms. The village had a drainage system and even indoor toilets.

The structures at Skare Brae were connected by a winding network of low narrow stone passage. It was therefore possible to travel from one house to another without having to step outside the complex. The passages were a little over a meter high (3¼ feet) and roofed with stone slabs which were covered over with insulating midden. The low height of the passages not only helped minimize drafts but could have served a symbolic, or possibly even a defensive, purpose forcing the one entering to stoop-over exposing themselves to retaliation.

One main passage led into the village with a bar-hole straddling the entrance. It shows that it could be sealed and visitors entering were forced, as stated, to kneel, or stoop to enter. Bar-holes were found along the length of the passages and also at the entrance of each house. The door to each of the dwellings consisted of a large slab of stone, big enough to fill the low entrance gap. When this was closed it was held in place by a bar slotted into the bar-holes.

Life in Skare Brae was probably secure and agreeable to the inhabitants. Examination of the midden shows that cattle and sheep formed the main diet, with barley and wheat grown in the surrounding fields.

Supplementing farm produce the midden indicates that fish and shellfish were collected and possibly kept fresh in custom stone tanks within the dwellings. Red deer and boar were also hunted for their meat and skins along with seal meat.[7]

What happen to Skare Brae? Changing Neolithic society brought about different ideas, values and way of life. From later and larger Neolithic structures in the area we see the emergence of an elite ruling body who had the power to control the labor of people. Individuals became part of larger communities with an increase specialization and led by tribal or spiritual leaders. The need for all-enclosed village communities were disappearing and the time period for families depending on their tight-knit, village areas were no longer needed. Skare Brae's demise was certainly not overnight.

Overtime families just dispersed across the landscape, settling once again in single individual dwellings. Younger people drifted from the villages and those who remained within the ancient village of Skare Brae gradually grew older and died.

Skare Brae & Earth 20 kyaBp: Skare Brae has taught us a number of factors. We find much of a previous civilization's existence is hidden from us; no one knew about Skare Brae until it was uncovered by storms. This situation points to being naive concerning past civilizations/societies and our ignorance of what has been lost because of sea-level rise and erosion.

The last few chapters have reviewed the recent historical scholarship and archaeological investigations on prehistorical sites. This is based on current distribution of global land and water which has existed for the last 10,000 years. Contemporary archaeology therefore examines land currently above sea level or within diving range (100 feet depending on equipment).

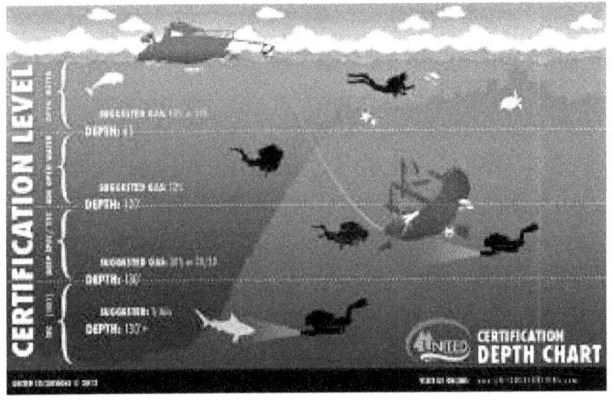

However, 20 kyaBp earth looked entirely different. Viewing current population maps, we find that the bulk of humanity lives along ocean, lake coasts or along rivers. The reasons for this are obvious and supported by archaeology and history. Throughout time rivers gave access to food and water consumption needed for survival. It was used as defense in protecting a military unit's flanks in battle or as moats around a castle or manner houses. The fact remans that the majority of earth's population lived along water. Rivers, oceans and large lakes were used for transportation and trading

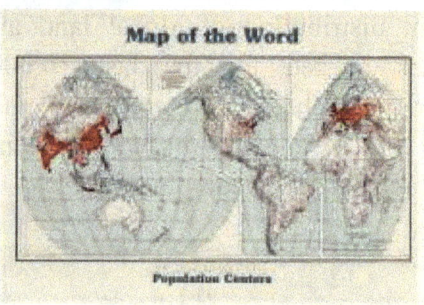

which is still true to the present day. Although railroads and overland highway routes have taken the bulk of shipping and transportation there are still items moved today by canals. Examples of major shipping and transportation canals today include the Suez Canal, the Kiel Canal, the Panama Canal and even New York State's Erie/Barge Canal.

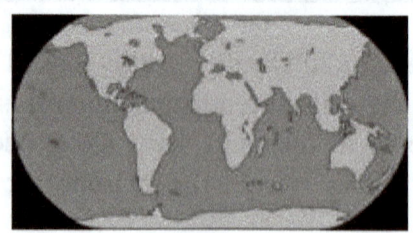

As stressed, before 20 kyaBp the earth looked incredibly different even though the continents were in their present position. Sea levels were much lower, and more land was exposed. Consequently, populations centers were concentrated closer to prehistoric shorelines.

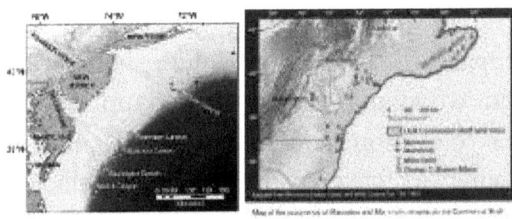

Those who lived in these communities fished, hunted, and possibly farmed. If they didn't farm, they would have foraged in similar locations for berries and tubers much as we would today. Further, they would have had shelters placed in an area that was close to water, and certainly semi-permanent in Northern climates. It could be imagined that their dwellings were similar to those that were found in the Neolithic period in Europe.

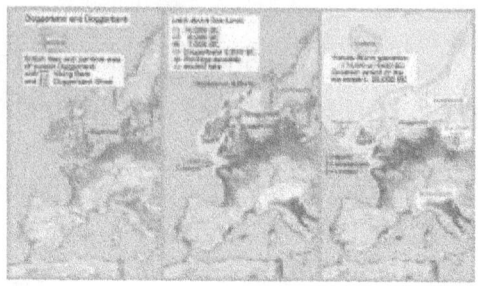

Climate and typography are other changes that are apparent. The continental shelf was well watered woodland and continued up through the "higher' elevations via river valleys and canyons. The source of these rivers were huge glacier lakes such as Lake Agassiz, or Glacial Lake Wisconsin.

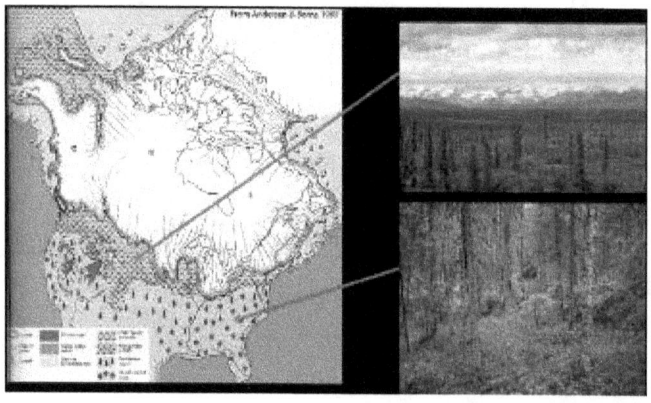

Considering differences in water level and climate there is a large number of possible archaeological sites that are inaccessible today. It's as though the USA was flooded, and archaeologists were investigating Long Lake, NY; Richwood, West Virginia; Moab, Utah; and Mackay, Idaho and using their finds to write the history of the USA. There is evidence that needs to be examined to get a better handle on pre-history and what occurred 20kyaBp.

Chapter 3
The Younger Dryas Cataclysmic Event and the End of Prior Civilizations?

Anyone who grew up in one of the three great mutually exclusive Western Civilization Religions (Judaism, Islam, or Christianity) have heard of Noah's Ark and the Great Flood. Many say it's a nice story, or it could never happen, and of course what happened to the Unicorns? The fact is even though the story seems at the very least mythical there are numerous stories of floods found around the world. They are not all identical, but they are all similar in that a great flood was coming, a special person was warned by a god(s), or divine/ semi-divine visitor, then they built a boat and saved some part of civilization.

The fact that there are a great number of flood stories from multiple cultures points to something that must have occurred in antiquity to have this impact. Below is a partial list of recorded flood events with a closer investigation of several of the more well-known ones.

- North America
  - Haisla, Kitimat (Kwinageese), Atnarko, Nootka Sound Tahsees, Central Kitimat, Tlingit Kitimat (Anyx Atnax), Revillant Island Tahsees, Seward Tahsees, Greenlander
  - Tlingit (southern Alaska coast), Squirlies (Alaska), Tsimsh (Alaska and south), Lowriners (Border Columbia, Puget) and Sknet (Puget tribes), Katka (northern inland British Columbia), Thompson Indian (British Columbia), Sarcee (Alberta), Tentant
  - Skidii, Queen Charlotte Is., British Columbia, Tsimshian (British Columbia)
  - Kwakiutl (British Columbia)
  - Kootenay (southwest British Columbia), Squamish (British Columbia), Belly Creek (British Columbia), Lillooet (lower River, British Columbia), Makah (Cape Flattery, Washington), Kalliam interference, Washington), Skhkomish (Washington), Skagit (Washington), Quileyute (Washington), Nisqually (Washington), Twana, Puget Sound, Washington), Kallisant
  - Coastal Mountains
  - Apokamak Nez Perce, Cayuse (eastern Washington), Yakama (Washington), White Springs (Oregon), Jicarra (northern Oregon), Sake River (northern California coast), Winnt (north central California), Huchi (coastal California), Southern Miwok (central California), Tuloreman Miwok (near Clear Lake, California), Tlamouka Miwok (Bodega Bay, California)/(Santa Clan Francisco in western, California)
  - Los Aibahuenza County, California
  - Ruuta (northern California interior), Pomo (north central California), Salinan (California), Yana (western Arizona, northern California), Havasupai (lower Colorado River)
  - Lake Indian, California
  - Yurok (north California coast), Blackfoot (Alberta and Montana), Cree (Canada), Chippewa-Ojibway (Canada), Chippewa (Ontario, Minnesota, Wisconsin), Ottawa, Menomee/Winnewe, Michigan, Mantee, Cherokee (Minnesota), Yellowstone, Chinquapin (northern Gulf of St. Lawrence), Mettawe (eastern Maritime Canada), Algonquian (upper Ottawa River), Lenape (Delaware), Delaware (to New York)
  - Cherokee Abara (also area, eastern Tennessee)
  - Mandan (North Dakota), Lakota
  - Chocsaw (Mississippi), Natchez (Lower Mississippi)
  - Chitimacha (Southern Louisiana)
  - Caddo (Oklahoma, Arkansas), Pawnee (Nebraska)
  - Navajo (Four Corners area), Apache (northeastern New Mexico)
  - San Juan River Arizona
  - Acoqchimese (near San Juan Capistrano, California), Luiseño (Southern California), Pima (southwest Arizona), Papago (Arizona), Hopi (northeast Arizona), Zuni (New Mexico)

- Central America
  - Tarascan (northern Michoacan, Mexico), Michoac-an (Mexico)
  - Yaqui (Sonora), Northern Nlavato, Tlaxcalapa (Northern Mexico), Huichol (western Mexico), Cora (west of the Huichol), Tepacane (southwest of the Huichol), Teputhan (central Mexico), Tohri (Jalisco), Nahua (central Mexico), Tarahum (central Mexico)
  - Tlapaneca (south central Mexico), Mixtec (northern Oaxaca, Mexico), Zapotec (Oaxaca, southern Mexico), Triqui (Oaxaca southern Mexico)
  - Totonac (eastern Mexico)
  - Chol (southern Mexico), Tzeltal (Chiapas, southern Mexico), Quiche (Guatemala), Maya (southern Mexico and Guatemala)
  - Popoluca (Veracruz, Mexico)
  - Nicaragua, Panama
  - Carib (Antilles)

- South America
  - Arawac (Guiana), Arekena (Guiana), Maturdas (Venezuela), Macusi (British Guyana)
  - Muisca (Colombia), Yanam (southern Venezuela)
  - Venezuelan (southern Venezuela)
  - Tucanoman (Guiana), Arawak (Guiana), Panam-, Macheo, and Ramelei (Puen R., Brazil), Iparuna (Upper Amazon), Arajes (eastern, Ecuador), Shuar (Andes)
  - Macato (eastern Ecuador)
  - Calumi (Quito, Ecuador)
  - Guanta and Chuquito (Peru)
  - Atacamenoe (near Cuzco, Peru), Chavin (Quechua, Quechua, Inca (Peru), Colla (high Andes)
  - Chiriguano (southeast Bolivia)
  - Charrue (Eastern Paraguay)
  - Eastern Brazil (Rio de Janeiro region), Eastern Brazil (Cape Frio region), Caricu (Araguaia River, central Brazil), Conuato (south Brazil)
  - Araucania (coastal Chile)
  - Toba (northern Argentina)
  - Selk'nam (southern tip of Argentina)
  - Yamana (Tierra del Fuego)

- Australia
  - Arnhem Land (northern Territory)
  - Maung (Goulburn Islands, Arnhem Land), Gunwinggu (northern Arnhem Land)
  - Gunwinggu (Arnhem Land)
  - Murgin (Arnhem Land)
  - Fitzroy River area (Western Australia)
  - Australian: Mount Elliot (coastal Queensland), Western Australia, Antakarinya (South Australia), Wirangu (South Australia), Narrinyeri (South Australia), Victoria, Lake Tyers/Victoria, Kurnai (Gippsland, Victoria), southeast Australia
  - Maori (New Zealand)
- Pacific Islands
  - Kabadi (New Guinea), Valman (northern New Guinea), Mamberao River (Irian Jaya), Samo-Kubo (western Papua New Guinea), Papua New Guinea
  - Palau Islands (Micronesia), western Carolines
  - New Hebrides, Lifou (one of the Loyalty Islands), Fiji
  - Samoa, Nanumanga (Tuvalu, South Pacific), Mangaia (Cook Islands), Rakaanga (Cook Islands), Raiatea (Leeward Group, French Polynesia), Tahiti, Hawaii

The Great Flood of Gun-Yu circa 2200-2300 BCE (from Antiquity): The Great Flood of Gun-Yu was major flood in ancient China that lasted for two generations. People were displaced because of the flood along with famine and other storms. The people ran to the hills and mountains to escape. The

flood wasn't seen as a retribution from 'God' but a natural disaster. The story emphasizes the heroic efforts of people to alleviate the catastrophe and protect others.

Sumerian Flood myth. Earliest existing version of the poem circa 2000 BCE: The Sumerian hero, Gilgamesh, traveled the world in search of a way to cheat death. On one of his journeys, he came across an old man, Utnapishtim, who told Gilgamesh a story from centuries past. He said that because the gods were angry with humanity and wanted to destroy them, the gods

brought on a great flood. The god Ea, warned Utnapishtim and instructed him to build an enormous boat to save himself, his family, and "the seed of all living things." He does so, and the gods brought rain which caused the water to rise for many days. When the rains subsided, the boat landed on a mountain, and Utnapishtim set loose first a dove, then a swallow, and finally a raven, which found land. The god Ishtar created the rainbow and placed it in the sky, as a reminder to the gods and a pledge to mankind that there would be no more floods.

The discovery of artifacts associated with Aga and Enmebaragesi of Kish, two other kings named in the stories, has lent credibility to the historical existence of Gilgamesh.[8]

***Hebrew Flood myth circa 500 BCE (from Antiquity)*:** God saw how great wickedness had become and decided to wipe humanity off the face of the earth. But one righteous man among all the people of that time, Noah, was found in God's favor. With specific instructions God told Noah

to build an ark for him and his family in preparation for a catastrophic flood that would destroy every living thing on earth. God further instructed Noah to bring into the ark two of all living creatures, both male and female, and seven pairs of all the clean animals, along with food for the animals. After Noah and his family had entered the ark, rain fell for a period of forty days and nights (all the springs of the vast watery deep burst open and the floodgates of the heavens were opened). The waters flooded the earth for a hundred and fifty days, and every living thing was destroyed. As the waters receded, the ark came to rest on the mountains of Ararat.[9]

***Namu Doryeong myth. Legend of Great Flood, Korea (from Antiquity)*:** Namu Doryeong was the son of a beautiful celestial woman and an ancient tree god, and when he was a young child his mother returned to the heavens and left him on earth with his father. Soon after, it began to rain heavily for many days, and soon all the land was beneath the water, so the father-tree called out to his son and told him to climb onto his branches. Namu Doryeong was safe from drowning, but he saw that other creatures were in danger. As Namu and his father floated along the raging waters, the young child saved a family of ants, a cloud of mosquitoes and eventually a human child that cried for help from the waves below. Namu Doryeong begged his father to let them save the boy, but his father-tree warned him '*Do as you wish, I leave it up to you, but you will regret saving him.*'

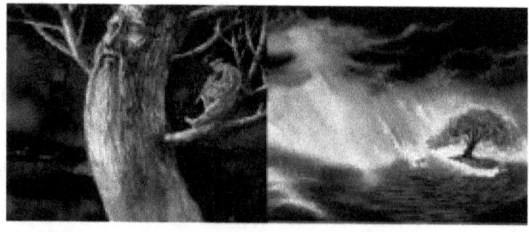

Eventually they landed on an island that was made up of the peak of Mt. Baekdu, the highest mountain in Korea, and there they found an old woman and two young girls who had survived the rains.

The old woman said that if Namu Doryeong won a contest, then he and the young boy he saved could marry the two girls. As the tale goes, with the assistance of the ants and mosquitoes he saved, Namu Doryeong won the contest and together the two couples formed the next race of humans.

Shatapatha Brahmana, the Flood of Manu. Hindu flood saga written 300 BCE (from Antiquity): In the Manu flood myth, Manu was brought to earth by the gods as the first man on earth. One day when he was washing his hands in a bowl of water, he saw a small Fish that told him a flood was coming and he needed to build a boat. On the boat, Manu was to bring two of every kind of animal and two of every kind of plant seed. The Fish added that when the flood came, he would help Manu.

Manu then kept the Fish in a fish tank, and it kept getting bigger and bigger to the point where he had to throw it in the ocean. Soon after the flood came, Manu entered the boat alone and tied a rope to the horn of the Fish and it guided him through the rough waves of the storm, leading him to the Himalayan mountains where they would part ways. Soon after the gods blessed him with a wife and they soon started to re populate the world.

Plato's Atlantis Myth, circa 360 BCE (from Antiquity): The story of Atlantis comes from two Socratic dialogues called *Timaeus* and *Critias* The dialogues discuss Socrates' request for three men to meet him. These were Timaeus of Locri, Hermocrates of Syracuse, and Critias of Athens. Socrates asked the men to tell him stories concerning how ancient Athens interacted with other states. Critias was first and told how his grandfather had met with the Athenian poet and lawgiver Solon who was elected to office in 594 BCE to reform the Athenian government. He refused to be a Tyrant or form a Tyranny but did establish a constitution.

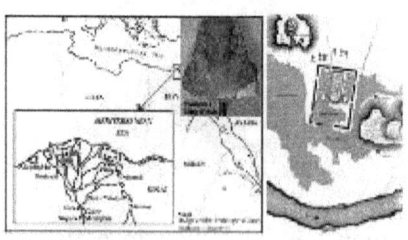

Solon had been to Egypt where an aged Priests from the Temple of Sais. The Priest had compared Egypt and Athens and talked about the gods and legends of both lands. One such Egyptian story was about Atlantis.[10]

Plato's Atlantis Myth-Timaeus Dialogue: Crossing the outer harbors, which were three in number, you would come to a wall which began at the sea and went all round: this was everywhere distant fifty stadia from the largest zone and harbor, and enclosed the whole, meeting at the mouth of the channel toward the sea. The entire area was densely crowded with habitations; and the canal and the largest of the harbors were full of vessels and merchants coming from all parts, who, from their numbers, kept up a [countless] sound of human voices and din of all sorts night and day.

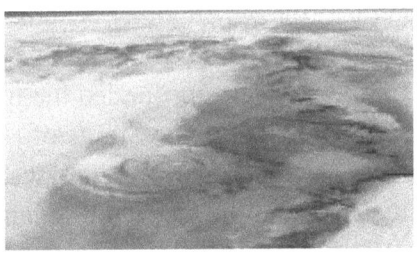

I have repeated his descriptions of the city and the parts about the ancient palace nearly as he gave them, and now I must endeavor to describe the nature and arrangement of the rest of the country. The whole country was described as being very lofty and precipitous on the side of the sea, but the country immediately about and surrounding the city was a level plain, itself surrounded by mountains which descended toward the sea; it was smooth and even, but of an oblong shape, extending in one direction three thousand stadia, and going up the country from the sea through the center of the island two thousand stadia; the whole region of the island lies toward the south, and is sheltered from the north (Appendix 1).[11]

Plato's Atlantis Myth-Critias Dialogue: This power came forth out of the Atlantic Ocean, for in those days the Atlantic was navigable; and there was an island situated in front of the straits which you call the Columns of Heracles (the Strait of Gibraltar, known as the Pillars of Hercules): the island was larger than Libya and Asia (Turkey) put together, and was the way to other islands, and from the islands you might pass through the whole of the opposite continent which surrounded the true ocean; for this sea which is within the Straits of Heracles is only a harbor, having a narrow entrance, but that other is a real sea, and the surrounding land may be most truly called a continent.

Now, in the island of Atlantis there was a great and wonderful empire, which had rule over the whole island and several others, as well as over parts of the continent; and, besides these, they subjected the parts of Libya within the Columns of Heracles as far as Egypt, and of Europe as far as Tyrrhenia (Italy). . . But afterward there occurred violent fancible earthquakes and floods, and in a single day and night of rain all your warlike men in a body sunk into the earth, and the island of Atlantis in like manner disappeared, and was sunk beneath the sea (Appendix 1).[12]

Flood Stories Discounted: Flood stories are discounted for a number of reasons. Most see these stories as either myths or folklore and give them little credibility. Those who do believe in an actual flood typically are taking it by faith though divine writings or else inspiration from a psychic or religious prophet. Therefore, the flood event occurs not because of natural causes, these may be used, but because humanity has displeased God/Supreme

Being by not obeying their commands, practicing wicked actions, blasphemy, etc.

Many times, the story isn't given any credibility because the description doesn't seem plausible. An example is the size of the Ark compared to modern ships.

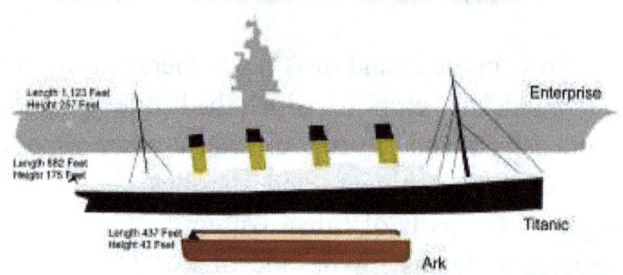

This doesn't affect the faith-based believers, however, the historian, archaeologist, even the geologist discards the stories as untrue or allegorical and fancible.

An additional problem with the stories is the locations of where the myths took place are either not discernable or are embellished to a point that someone couldn't locate it on a map. Further myths tend to be ethnocentric and lead to a rebirth of a particular society leaving sister societies unknown.

These ancient stories are of course verbal and there is a tendency not to consider oral traditions as a viable resource. The fact that many times there are allegorical aspects of the myth results in doubting the possible viable aspects of the event. Finally, It's just fiction, a nice made-up story to entertain guests. Yet, made-up stories at times seem to have a ring of truth.

In 1346 news reached Europe of a terrible plague devastating the East. According to the Chronicler of Este: "Between Cathay and Persia there rained a vast rain of fire; falling in flakes like snow or burning up mountains and plains and other lands, with men and women; and then arose vast masses of smoke; and whosoever beheld this died within the space of half a day; and likewise, any man or woman who looked upon those who had seen this."[13]

What plague was being described here? The Bubonic Plague, very real and killing the majority of those who contracted it. In Europe they didn't say it was a rain of fire, but, God, or possibly comets, alignment of the planets and of course the Jewish people were always part of the blamed.

Regardless, the plague was real and killed up to 50% of Europe. An historic event that certainly occurred.

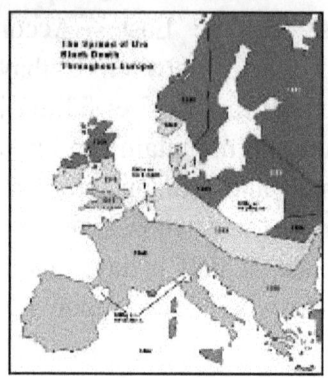

The Plague was near enough to our time period to be remembered and the allegory understood. When we read about a flood from antiquity there are no later interpretations. Possibly because of the length of time since the event occurred, or the problem of enormous devastation and perhaps there were few if any written records that survived.

So, what then, should we just disregard all of these tales. People from around the world, from both hemispheres, have narratives, parables, and folktales concerning a massive flood, that to those involved was the whole world, with someone escaping. Either a single person, or a family, or an area, fleeing a disaster. What event could have happened around 12 kya that changed history?

The Younger Dryas Period: The Younger Dryas is known as one of the best examples of abrupt climate change. Around 14.5 kya, the climate started to swing from a "cold glacial world to a warmer interglacial one." As this change was occurring the temperatures in the Northern Hemisphere abruptly resumed near-glacial conditions. "This near-glacial period is called the Younger Dryas, named after a flower, *Dryas Octopetala*, that grows in cold conditions and that became common in Europe during this time."[14] Approximately 11.5 kya the Younger Dryas ended particularly abruptly. Greenland temperatures after a decade rose 10°C (18°F). This was found in other records, including varved lake sediments in Europe.[15]

The Younger Dryas is clearly detectable in paleoclimate records from around the world. An example would be the Cariaco Basin north of Venezuela where temperatures decreased about 3°C (5.5°F). Some of this cooling could have been owed to greater upwelling of cooler subsurface water. Parts of the Northern Hemisphere tropics found conditions becoming drier.[16] The question then becomes, what caused the Younger Dryas Period and what was its effect?

Younger Dryas Area Boundary: When we investigate the region of this event, we notice an area that was substantially disturbed. The map below illustrates the area of the Younger Dryas Boundary. The field shows YDB investigation sites as dots. From the study's investigation, evidence was found of a large impact had occurred of sufficient strength to wipe out animal and human life within the area.

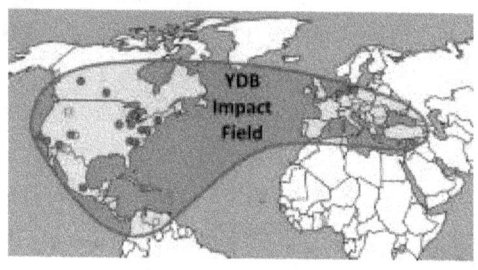

The map shows "24 sites containing Younger Dryas Boundary (YDB) nano-diamonds. The solid line defines the current known limits of the YDB field of cosmic-impact proxies, spanning 50 million km^2, including Venezuela"[17]

Why? What was the Cause? The Younger Dryas Boundary Impact Field: There have been many theories concerning the cause of the Younger Dryas Period. Some have hypothesized that a solar activity was involved, others felt that meteoric activity caused the event. However, the proponents lacked evidence of a meteor impact. They theorized that a large Tunguska type event might have occurred that didn't leave a crater.

In 2018 the Hiawatha crater, in Greenland was discovered. The crater is one of the 25 largest craters on earth (19 miles in diameter and 1,050 ft in depth). Based on the size of the crater, it's estimated the asteroid would have been around ¾ of a mile across and would have weighed 11 to 12 billion tons as it entered the atmosphere. The impact would have been so great it would have vaporized the asteroid.[18] This doesn't negate a large Tunguska type event was additionally involved, however, the crater points to a massive "hard rock" meteor striking the planet and causing an enormous amount of destruction.

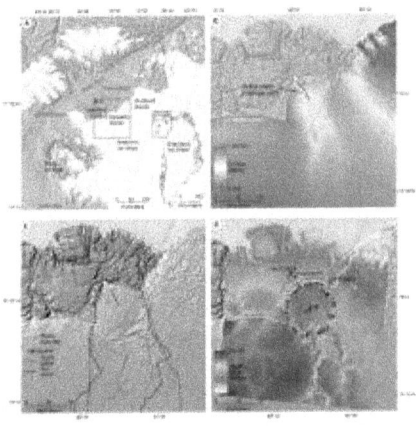

The asteroid's impact released the power of nearly 4 billion pound-force. In comparison a 100 megaton-bomb has about 221 million pound-force and the atomic bomb used on Hiroshima; 15

kilotons had .0033 million pound-force. Hiroshima destroyed over 8 square-miles of the city and 180,000 people died.

Result of the Incident? The Younger Dryas Boundary Impact Field: The meteor strike would have devastated the Northern Hemisphere especially the arctic with a rippling affect around the world. The impact would be devastating the ice-covered land masses, vaporizing millions of tons of ice, water and bedrock, hurling it into the atmosphere and ejecting it out of the impact area. The ejecta would have included both large boulders and chunks of ice. It would have created huge tsunamis that reached outside the impact field carrying debris and rafting large pieces of shattered ice and stone. These tsunamis would have crossed the Atlantic destroying everything along the coastlines and waterways that emptied into the Atlantic.

For a comparison, a review of the Boxing Day 2004 Indian Ocean earthquake and tsunami is instructional. A 9.1 magnitude quake along a fault off Sumatra Island, Indonesia created a massive tsunami. Within 20 minutes a series of 100-foot waves hit the shoreline of Banda Aceh and destroyed the city killing more than 100,000 people. The quake itself released the equivalent of 23,000 Hiroshima-type atomic bombs. This would be the equivalent of a 345 megaton-bomb and would create about 763 million pound-force. The tsunamis traversed the Indian Ocean at 500 mph causing a shift in the Earth's mass which changed the planet's rotation. Eight hours after the earthquake the tsunami hit the coast of Africa (Somalia, Tanzania, and Kenya) killing 300 people.[19]

The Hiawatha asteroid's impact released about 4 billion pound-force with a tsunami that could have ranged from 1 to 2 miles deep moving at 500 mph.

The distance between the Greenland impact area and northwest Africa is approximately 4300 miles and 3700 miles from Baffin Bay to Africa.

The tsunami from the Indonesian to Africa traveled 3700 miles and caused devastation. Imagine the Hiawatha tsunami at least 1mile deep striking the African coast devastating it and moving inland with any debris destroying everything in its path.

In North America, the Hiawatha meteor impacted not just topography but permanently changed the life cycle of, or eliminated altogether, many of the animals indigenous to the continent including modern humans.

Because of the orientation of the earth 12 kya and a general warming of the planet it's believed there were large inland lakes of meltwater held back by giant ice dams. The meteor impact would have released these huge inland lakes changing the landscape and emptying eventually into the ocean and ultimately impacting world currents, salinity and rise in water level. Lake Agassiz for example covered an area of roughly 365,000 square miles.

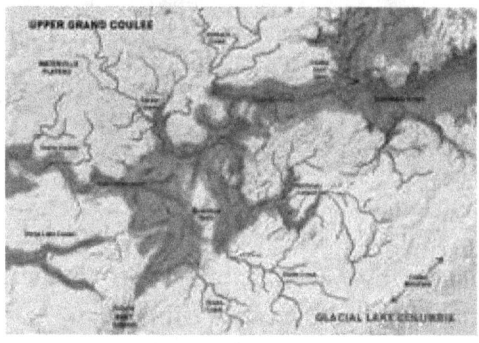

The Hiawatha asteroid's impact affected land animals, modern humans and caused a change in the topography and shifting of river courses across the land leading to a number of natural occurrences coming together. The first is the meteor(s) striking the earth and its results. Around the same time there was a climatic change occurring. This climatic shift was occurring because of the precession of the earth. It takes 26000 years for the earth rotational axis to precesses one revolution.

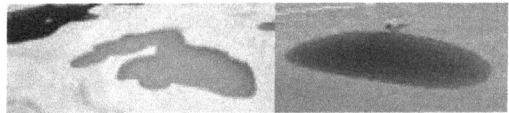

Therefore about 12 kya the North Pole wasn't pointing at Polaris but Vega. This permitted large meltwater lakes to form in North America and allowed what is often called the "Green Sahara" across northern Africa to occur. When the meteor(s)

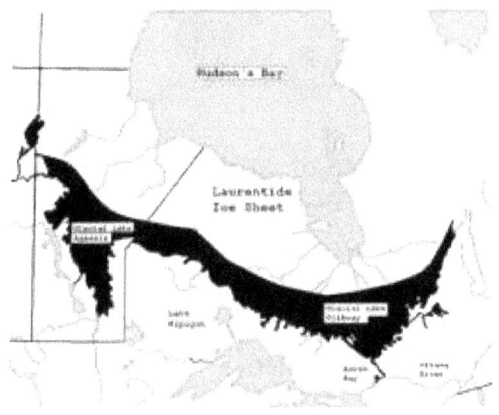

hit trillions of gallons of water were released either from a direct hit or from the substantial earthquakes following the strike.

***Green* Sahara:** The African Humid Period illustrates the extraordinary climate shifts that the planet encounters as a result of subtle variations in the Earth's orbit. The "greening" Sahara not only symbolizes a remarkable conversion of the hydrologic cycle, but evidence also shows that gradual climate break down can result in rapid climate responses.[20]

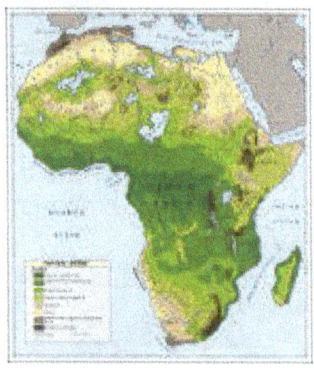

The abundance of North African paleoclimate and archeological records emphasizes the essential value of water accessibility on sustainability and people, and the central role of climate in shaping major events in social development leading to the rise of dense, urban societies.[21]

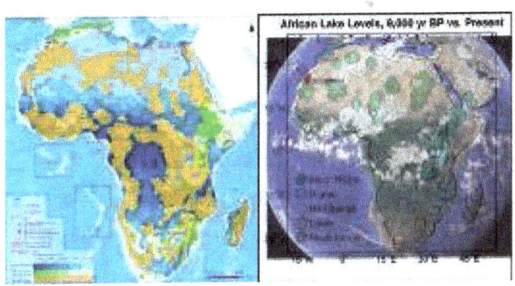

The Earth's axial spin is disturbed by gravitational interactions with the moon and the gigantic planets that together make periodic changes in the Earth's orbit, including "a 100,000-year cycle in the shape of the orbit (eccentricity), a 41,000-year cycle in the tilt of the Earth's axis (obliquity) and a 20,000-year cycle in the "wobble," much like a top's wobble on the Earth's axis (precession)."[22]

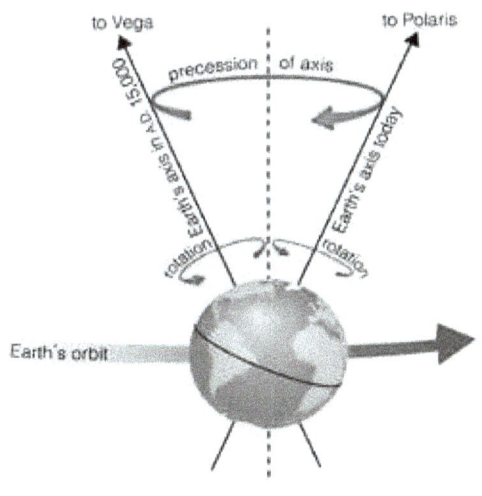

All three of orbital cycles called *Milankovitch cycles* impact African climate on long geologic timescales, but the cycle with the most influence on the rains in Africa is the "wobble" cycle, precession. The central climatic result of precession is to alter the season when Earth has its closest pass to the Sun (perihelion) called the precession of the equinoxes. Today, perihelion happens in northern hemisphere winter but at 10,000 years ago (half of a precession cycle) it transpired in the northern hemisphere summer, and summer radiation over North Africa was about 7% higher than it is today.[23]

Atlantis – What do we know? When we start to do research on Atlantis it is crucial to purge superfluous & specious sources of evidence, and just as important to know it was a real location. Herodotus knew Atlantis was real and detailed the site of it on a 450 BCE map of the world.

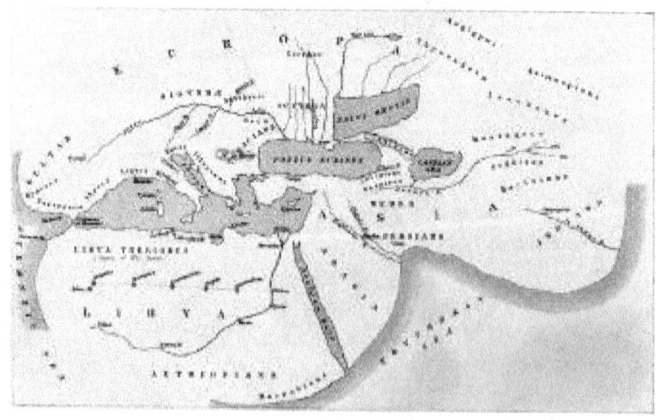

Prior to Herodotus there were others who spoke of a rich circular city. Homer in the 8th century BCE, Hesiod in the 7th century BCE, Pindar and Hellanicus in the 5th century BCE. All of them spoke of a similar location. Plato, a hundred years

after Herodotus, describes Atlantis in his Socratic dialogues *Timaeus* & *Critias* written in 360 BCE.

Atlantis – What are we told? Plato tells us most of the details that are used in descriptions of the island of Atlantis. He writes that Atlantis was a great and amazing empire and ruled over the whole island and several others nearby and parts of the continent. Plato wrote that they subjected the parts of Libya within the Columns of Heracles, as far as Egypt, and of Europe as far as Tyrrhenia (Italy).

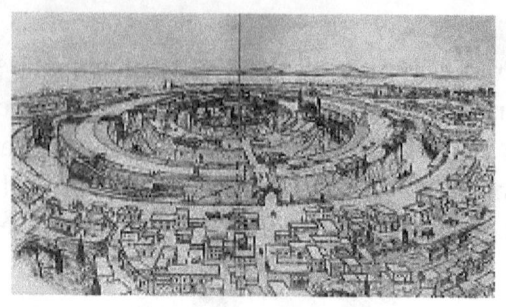

In another passage Plato writes that the Atlanteans ruled in the center of the whole island, and that there was an extremely fertile plain surrounding it. He also wrote that fifty stadia from the center of the island, was a low mountain range surrounding the plain.

Diameter Central Island with Royal Palace	5 Stade*	3035-3150 ft.
Outer Diameter of Inner Water Ring	7 Stade	4249-4410 ft.
" " " Inner Land Ring	13 Stade	4677-4830 ft.
" " " Middle Water Ring	15 Stade	9105-9450 ft.
" " " Outer Land Ring	21 Stade	2.41-2.5 miles
" " " Outer Water Ring	27 Stade	3.1-3.22 miles
Outer City Wall bordering the Sea Diameter	127 Stade	14.6-15.15 miles
Length	400 Stade	45.68-48 miles

*1 Stade = 607-630 ft

Atlantis – Where is it? Many have placed Atlantis everywhere from the Caribbean to the Mediterranean and of course in the middle of the Atlantic. There have been psychics who have described what it was like to live there and others who believe it's from another dimension. However, certainly Herodotus' map would give a clue. When we look at the location and look at this part of Africa from space, we find something interesting.

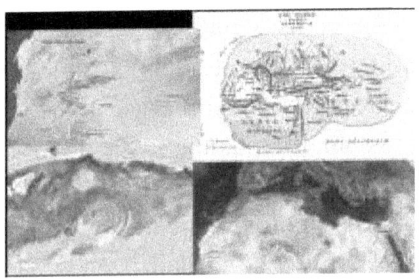

From looking at the Herodotus' Map and at arial photography we find that where Herodotus' map points to Atlantis is where we find what is known as the *Eye of Africa* or properly known as the *Richat Structure*. Looking straight down at the feature we find something that meets the general description and typical visualization of Atlantis. Surprisingly, the dimensions of the *Richat Structure* match the dimensions claimed by Plato's Atlantis.

Not only does the *Richat Structure* match in shape, but there is a great deal of evidence that at one time the area had a large amount of water either an inland lake or as a part of a large river system which had lakes within it such as the St. Lawrence River with Trois Riviéres on Lac Saint-Pierre.

There is an abundance of evidence that the region had a substantial quantity of water and that looking at aerial photos you can see what appears to be the topography of land had been drained after a big wave impacted it. In fact, upon closer inspection

we see a number of items. It's easy to notice the continental shelf is narrower there than anywhere else in the area and even with a lower sea level it would not add a lot of land area. Looking further we

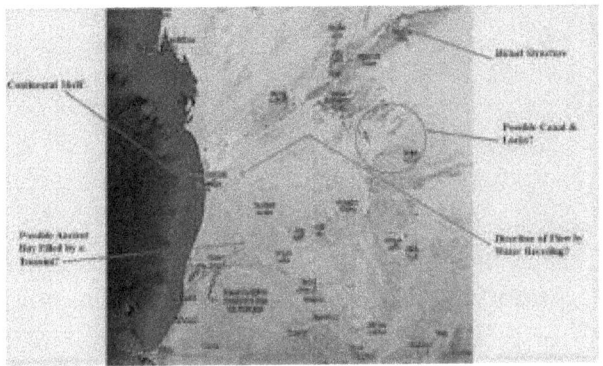

observed the direction of apparent drainage from a tsunami with evidence of mollusks in the debitage of the region. Finally, we notice what could have been a canal, possibly with locks.

There is also a detectable area that could have been a large bay before it was destroyed by a tsunami. This isn't that far-fetched of an idea when we consider the changes of the Persian Gulf since approximately 5000 BCE.

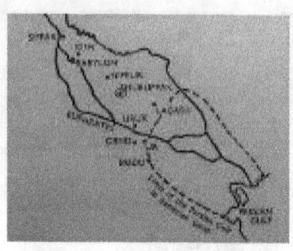

Atlantis – Location Geology: When people visit or think about New York City they think of Manhattan Island. The thoughts of Time Square, Washington Park fill the mind. If someone considers it in an historic sense the Collect Pond or maybe the old city of New Amsterdam could come to mind. The Island of Manhattan is a naturally made island that was modified by humans. Imagine what it would look like 12,000 years after a catastrophe.

Was the *Richat Structure* naturally made through diapirism and later modified? Diapirism

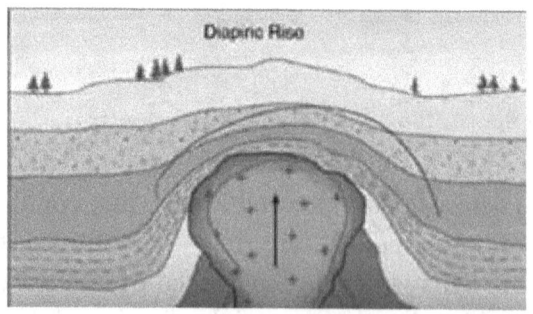

is caused by a fairly mobile mass that intrudes into preexisting rocks. Diapirs commonly intrude vertically through more dense rocks because of buoyancy forces associated with relatively low-density rock types, such as salt, shale and hot magma. This causes diapirs to form.[24] The

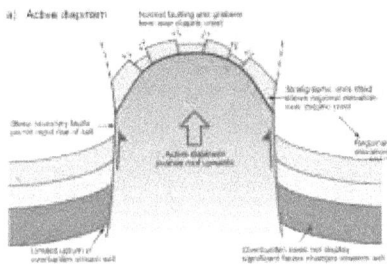

process is accomplished through the pushing upward and piercing overlying rock layers forming diapirs.

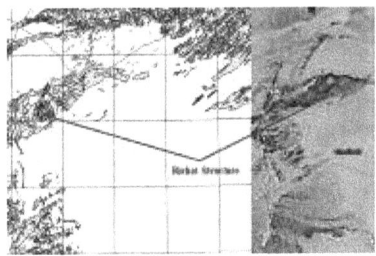

If this was found in an area that was well watered, along an inland sea and open to trade routes, such as Manhattan, people would have enlarged its natural harbors and using the raw material found there, constructed buildings, bridges, and ships. When this area was populated, it was a time when the climate could support various forms of vegetation, trees, and other natural resources.

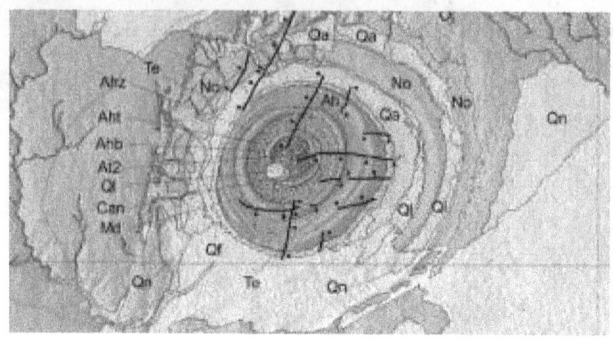

Chapter 4
Atlantis: What would it have been like?

So, two questions finally become apparent after examining all the all information from the previous chapters, what do we know about Atlantis, and do we know where it was? These questions have been attempted to be answered by numerous people through logic, history, or by 'spiritual' interaction. As for those who have written about Atlantis probably Edgar Cayce and his book *Edgar Cayce on Atlantis* by Warner Books in 1968 is the best known. Cayce's book discussions his versions of life though a self-induced trance and his belief in his various reincarnations.

Cayce details the timeline of Atlantis from 50 kya BCE to 10 kya BCE and regales us with its final destruction. While there are several other well-known authors, I would be remis not to mention Erich von Däniken, author of *Chariots of the Gods*, who wrote a book entitled *The Gods from Outer Space: Atlantis, Men and Monsters* giving his own twist on the subject.

Movies have contributed a great deal to the perception of Atlantis from *Queen of Atlantis*

(1932) to *Siren of Atlantis* (1949), even the Lego movie DC Comic *Superheroes: Aquaman - Rage of Atlantis* (2018 video). Video games also delve into the Atlantean mythos with games such as *Age of Mythology* (2002) where Arkantos heroic admiral of Atlantis interact with the Titans. This brings about conspiracy theories of all sorts. Such as, Atlantis was/is a secret Reptilian city that is under the surface of the earth all the way to the US Government's 1973 Pepperdine Atlantis Expedition.[25]

Not only are there countless ideas of Atlantis in book and film, there are nearly as many locations theorized. From the writings of Plato and literal interpretation of his writings most fix Atlantis in the middle of the Atlantic Ocean. Many point to the Rockcall bank and its unusual location and depth below sea level. Rockcall bank could have been an island chain at one time but doesn't really match the cities description. The Caribbean with its unique geological formation called the Bimini Road off Bahama is certainly an intriguing structure unfortunately it has been found to be a natural formation.

Many feel the Mediterranean Sea is another location for Atlantis. This comes from factors such as Plato miscalculated the size, or to some aspect fit what Plato wrote along with natural calamities. Many see Atlantis located on the volcanic island of Thera. When it erupted the blast destroyed Atlantis and the Minoan cities on Crete. The destruction was so great that there was no evidence of Atlantis left. Other areas that are near this part of the world include the Black Sea Floods that destroyed low-lying of cities and finally Cadiz, Spain and the Doñana National Park as a possible location.

Antarctica and the Amazon in South America are two other locations. Antarctica is a natural location since most of it is under thick ice or glaciers so that it is difficult to prove Atlantis isn't there. However, the conspiracy theories about Antarctica run wild from the home of a secret World War Two Nazi base to conspiracies that Antarctica has UFO sightings and with stories of UFO's leaving secret bases. All of this connected to Atlantis either still being in existence or in the case of the Nazis, the search for Atlantean technology.

South America and the Amazon basin have been offered as Atlantis. In recent years it has been discovered that the rain forest in the Amazon is a planned planting of trees, They found levees and causeways throughout the area with prepared soil. Investigations found a dark extremely artificially fertilized soil called Terra petra (anthropogenic), known as Indian Black Earth. Further, the Amazon basin was labelled as Atlantis on some older maps.

The above map of Atlantis Island or Atlantis Insula is by French cartographer Guillermo Sanson, 1661. It's one of many maps that depicts South America as Atlantis.

The fact is the *Richat Structure* fits neatly for location. Planning a journey from anywhere in the Mediterranean Sea area to the *Richat Structure* would require you to travel beyond the Pillars of Hercules. The final destination, the *Richat Structure* matches in appearance and location as described by Plato.

What Atlantis is not: We've touched on some of this before but there are a number of things that Atlantis is not. Atlantis isn't a landing zone for UFO's with giant pyramids releasing energy into the sky to communicate with other worlds or dimensions. We wouldn't find a typical modern city either with skyscrapers and large glass windows or classical Greco-Roman architecture. It must be remembered that Plato would have put a Greek cultural twist to the story which to some gives an imagined view of an ancient Greek civilization. There are those who will say if Atlanteans were so advanced why didn't they use metal, the answer could be simply, it wasn't necessary. If a society could carve and manipulate megalithic size rocks, why would they go to the trouble of manufacturing metals. A corollary would be those who participated in the Neolithic Revolution. Although large numbers eventually became Neolithic farmers, not all did. Those groups who could continue to be a hunter/gatherer society did so because all their needs were being met. An example of this is found in a dubious quote contributed to an American immigrant to Hawaii.

The ease with which the Hawaiians on their own land can secure their food supply has undoubtedly interfered with their social and industrial advancement. . . [It] relieves the native from any struggle and unfits him for sustained competition with men from other lands. The fact that food is supplied by nature takes from the native all desire for the acquisition of more land. Today's food can be had for the picking, and tomorrow's as well. Instead of grasping all he can get, he divides with his neighbor, and confidently expects his neighbor to divide with him.[26]

Although the quote is pejorative in nature it does point to the fact that it is supported.

The `ohana, or extended family, was the basic social unit of the Hawaiian community. Each `ohana lived and worked within land units, or `ili, within the larger ahupua`a land division. Most exchange and sharing of food, material goods, services or labor took place within the `ohana and operated more as a system of voluntary giving than of barter. The `ohana lived in kauhale, or clustered households, within short distance from fields and fishing grounds.[27]

This is an excellent example that people don't change unless they absolutely have too. Much like the Native Hawaiian, the ancient peoples would have continued using the abundant materials naturally occurring such as flint/chert, timber, stone, and natural adhesives (*e.g.,* birch-bark tar, pitch, plant resins and gums).

The other factor is that the tale of Atlantis is not a purely fictional story but undoubtedly contains truths hidden "between the lines." For centuries countless historians and archaeologists thought that the ancient City of Troy and the idea of the Trojan War was just a story. Then in 1868 Heinrich Schliemann found Troy right where it was thought to be located. Was there a Trojan horse, unknown, was there a type of deception of one sort used, we'll never know for sure? But he found Troy.

Heinrich Schliemann

It proved that Troy existed and the same could possibly be said about Atlantis. The story of Atlantis, even with exaggerations and metaphors has the same flavor as the story of the ancient City of Troy. It was seemingly just a story, but it contained truths about the past.

Archaeology of the Ancient City of Troy

Clues to Atlantis: There are a number of clues that an Atlantean empire was possible. One clue is the many megalithic and cyclopean structures that are of ancient ages and show remarkably similar building techniques. Examples are monuments, obelisks, and massive building block used in construction. Then there is the "coincidence" of pyramids being found throughout the world and almost on every continent. This points to a worldwide cultural knowledge of building techniques. Even the Sphinx's age is in contention with scholars pointing to water erosion on the walls surrounding the Sphinx, and the numerous repairs to the Sphinx that have been made over time. To some the Sphinx is at least 14,000 years old to 50,000 years old.[28]

We have a clue to Atlantis in the post YDP Event era, the Harappan/ Mohenjo-Daro society. The Harappan Society existed between 2500-1500 BCE and was immensely well organized. It's important to notice the modern comforts and similarities to our communities achieved without the use of materials in use today.

The cities had large lanes and side streets in a format you would see in most modern cities. They had running water, local wells and in some cases wells inside homes. The homes were in one- and

two-story designs with sewer systems for wastewater carrying it out of the city.

- 2500-1500 BCE
- over 1000 miles
  - worlds largest early civ
- Harappa and Mohenjo-Daro most important cities
  - capital cities
  - well organized gov'ts
  - checkered board pattern streets
  - walled fortress
  - supply warehouses
  - sewer system
  - taxed in form of food

Even more advanced is the described, and apparently archaeologically found, ancient sunken city of Dvārakā off the coast of India. Evidence

suggests that the area was above water prior to 9000 BCE with the National Institute of Ocean Technology establishing carbon-14 dates of 7500 to 9000 BCE for wood samples and pottery being dated to 3500 BCE. The city seems to have been advanced with city blocks and wide streets lined with single and multiple dwellings.[29]

Göbekli Tepe

Göbekli Tepe is another ancient site that demonstrates the sophistication of stonework dated to 11 kya. Excavations conducted in unique sections of Göbekli Tepe produced extraordinary megalithic architecture dated to the 12th and 11th millennia BCE. The Göbekli Tepe site contains massive, round stone structures and enormous stone pillars up to 5.5 m (18 ft) high. Interestingly, there was no evidence of farming or animal domestication.[30]

Sites such as Mohenjo-Daro, Dvārakā, and Göbekli Tepe indicate the complexity that was possible prior YDP Event in what has been described as an ancient techno-chalcolithic period.

Many people mistakenly perceive this time period of the "stone-age" as lacking tools that are versatile and reusable. Stone and bone tools were able to be fashioned into everything from bone needles, stone scrapers, projectile points to even knives. I've used modern knapped stone knives

at demonstrations and was able as to cut through plastic strapping and leather as easily as with any steel knife. The use of substances other than steel/metal for manufacturing tools may challenge our concepts of usability.

So, when we consider the possible technologies used at Atlantis, we need to shift our paradigm. Even the knowledge the ancient peoples were working with was of a different focus than ours. In fact, their science may look like magic as much as ours does to less sophisticated cultures. It is reported the Library of Alexandria had over 700,000 volumes of manuscripts from around the world dating back a thousand years. It contained texts of various languages & cultures, dictionaries, and "ancient" technologies that are based on different distinctives of physics than what we commonly use.

These technologies might include a number of different abilities. One of these, which can be replicated today is controlling manipulation of "stones" by the sun through the use of a parabolic mirror or lens. By using a solar apparatus and concentrating the sun on stone material, the material can be melted and shaped.

By heating lithic material, it could have been sculpted into megalithic blocks of various shapes

and sizes for building. Parabolic mirrors and lenses can generate temperatures up to 3800° Fahrenheit/ 2093° Celsius.[31] Temperatures in this range can melt Granite, which has a melting temperature of 2300° Fahrenheit/ 1260° Celsius.[32]

Theoretically, the temperature could be controlled so that Granite or other megalithic material such as Diorite or Andesite could be made pliable and shaped into blocks of various dimensions and shapes. Megalithic and Cyclopic

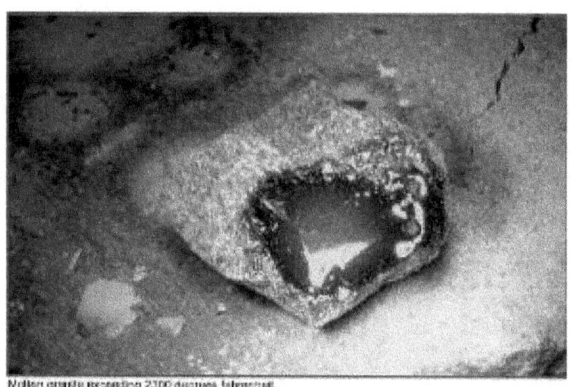

Molten granite exceeding 2300 degrees fahrenheit.

buildings show ample examples of holes, shafts and intricate building block designs all that could have done by this method.

CLASSIFICATION & FLOW CHARACTERISTICS OF VOLCANIC ROCKS

Basalt	Andesite	Dacite	Rhyolite	Volcanic rock name
40-52 %	52-63 %	63-68 %	68-77 %	Silica (SiO_2) content
1160°C			900°C	Eruption temperature Lava color scale in °C: 1160° 600°
Low resistance to flow (thin, runny lava)		High resistance to flow (thick, sticky)		Mobility of lava flows

Decreasing mobility of lava ⟶

It's also possible lithic material could be sliced using a tightly controlled narrow beam from a parabolic lens or mirror.

Summary Table

Magma Type	Solidified Volcanic Rock	Solidified Plutonic Rock	Chemical Composition	Temperature	Viscosity	Gas Content
Mafic or Basaltic	Basalt	Gabbro	45-55 SiO_2 %, high in Fe, Mg, Ca, low in K, Na	1000 - 1200 °C	Low	Low
Intermediate or Andesitic	Andesite	Diorite	55-65 SiO_2 %, intermediate in Fe, Mg, Ca, Na, K	800 - 1000 °C	Intermediate	Intermediate
Felsic or Rhyolitic	Rhyolite	Granite	65-75 SiO_2 %, low in Fe, Mg, Ca, high in K, Na	650 - 800 °C	High	High

Limestone begins to decompose at 1517° Fahrenheit/850° Celsius and this process could have been used to rough out large blocks, monoliths or even obelisks.

There is also evidence that using vibrations can aid in this process of cutting stone. Granite samples under ultrasonic vibration exhibited elastic-plastic distortion behavior. As the vibration continued, the deformation finally became ductile, and substantial division occurred.[33]

The creation of sawing tools using abrasives was possible. Experimentation has occurred demonstrating that copper or bronze types of saw apparatus with sand grit could cut stone. There is evidence of sawing of stone in stone quarries. Of course, they would have to move these cut blocks of granite and limestone.

The fact is the use of cranes and other machinery/technology could be completely possible during the "Atlantean" era. A Treadmill Crane could easily lift over 6 tons with two men in the "wheel." Additionally, levers and pullies would have been completely possible to position stones laterally.

13th Century Treadmill Crane

Certainly, the use of wooden ships is expected and along with ships would be shipping of raw materials and/or final products. The use of canals and locks would be further anticipated. In fact, as we shift our paradigm, hydraulic systems could also have been employed using mercury as hydraulic fluid instead of oil. Mercury has a number of interesting properties and has actually been found in large quantities below the Pyramid of the Feathered Serpent, third largest of the pyramids in Teotihuacan in central Mexico.

It has electrical conductivity properties naturally, but it can also be solidified at room temperature as a paste or solid when it is amalgamated with copper or any other metal and when mercury is mixed chemically with sodium produces hydrogen. An end product with many possibilities.

It's quite possible that this pre-Younger Dryas Period Event age could have been technologically advanced but not in the way we would expect.

Baghdad battery

Were there batteries or generators, certainly we have possible examples including the Baghdad battery for storage and we think of generators powered by wind or possibly an aeolipile type mechanism. (Figure below)

When you create electricity not only could you create some sort of arc-lamp but speakers using fire that could produce sound. Early in my career I was a project engineer designing sonar for nuclear attack submarines. I was reading a journal article one day

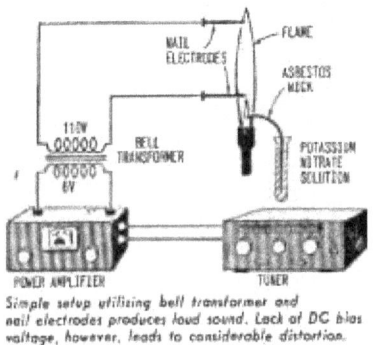

Flame Speaker Science Fair Project [34]

and it detailed flame producing sound when the impedance of the source is turned/tuned up. I immediately thought of Moses and the burning

bush. In retrospect now, I wonder, did Moses trigger an ancient recording? You can buy something similar today, known today as a plasma speaker.

It is not too much to assume that "Atlanteans" could have had working knowledge of analog computers such as a type of Antikythera Mechanism (below). The mechanism through gearing could follow movements of the Sun and Moon, predict eclipses, model the orbit of the Moon as well as other astronomical events.

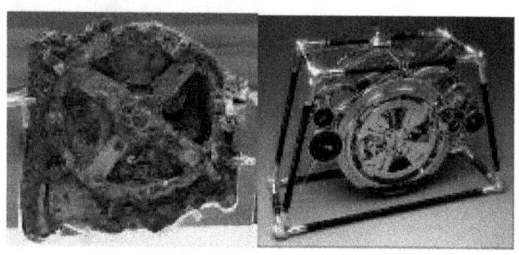

It would be believable that a society such as this would have comparable items such as slide-

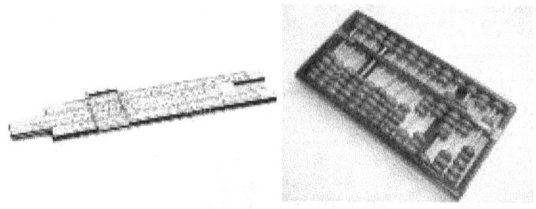

rules or abaci for calculation and a form of writing for communication and storing of scientific data.

Atlantis: So, with all of this information where and what was Atlantis? From written and archaeological investigations, we find that stone blocks were used to for building various structures both residential and commercial. Atlantis, from interpolation of Mesopotamian and Harrapan city structures, would have had city sewers and water.

While investigating Atlantis we need to shift our paradigm from our current technological solutions of observable needs to the possibilities of using something completely different to achieve the same or accomplish the need in a better way. There is no reason that there couldn't have been advanced Chalcolithic cultural metal working and even possibly the ability of alloying into bronze.

As for the city and its planning, it would not be surprising to have a sewer and water system possibly to every house. Electricity might have been a far reach, certainly steam and mechanical manipulation was possible.

We think of Heron of Alexandria and the prospects of his designs such as his aeolipile that demonstrated the prospect of steam and his famous automatic doors.

Could there have been a form of mass transportation similar to San Francisco's famous cable cars? Did Heron learn about these things while studying in the Library of Alexandria?

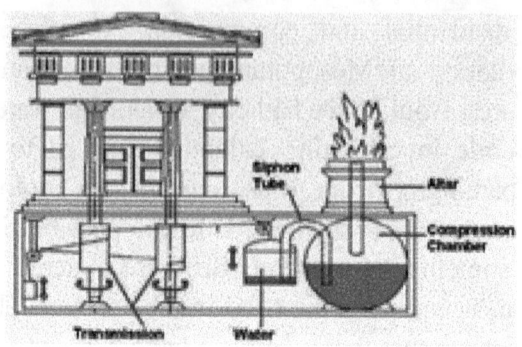

Heron of Alexandria's Automatic Doors

As indicated earlier, analog computers could also be part of this scenario. We think of the Antikythera mechanism and the possibilities that opens up for similar types of mechanisms that could compute various mathematic solutions. Certainly slide-rule technology wouldn't be outside the possibilities of this civilization.

So, where is all Atlantis' stuff? When discussing Atlantis absent of theories on spirituality/religion, nuances of government, or family/government dynamics the question comes up where are all Atlantean artifacts of this technology? Certainly, there must be remnants of the elaborate apparatuses which were used to melt stone, open & close automatic doors, audio speakers using fire to produce sound, shipping locks with canals, and a plethora of other technologies. So, simply speaking, where is all this stuff?

The absence of evidence can be summed up by three aspects that are interrelated. These are "the disaster" (YDP Event), the amount of time since "the disaster," and the changes in the sea level.

A "Hiawatha" type disaster, causing a change in the sea level, and over 12,000 years ago would certainly shift a great deal of topography and erase most of the evidence we would expect to find.

Even with ancient archaeological sites like those of the 40th century BCE such as Sumer in Mesopotamian, or Jiangzhai in China [roughly 6 kya] the evidence excavated gives a glimpse into the culture, and technology of the period. Items such as pottery, precious jewelry, grave sites and in some cases clay tablets with writing are found.

When investigating the disappearance of "Atlantean" evidence we have to factor in that we are exploring 12 kya, the 10th Millennium BCE. Under the best conditions most of the pottery/ utensils or jewelry may have decomposed completely. This corrosion would even be more prevalent for midden piles, animal bones, and certainly human burials. Add to this the extended period of time an "Hiawatha" type disaster lasted and even more evidence could be lost.

The Greenland Hiawatha meteor strike and the magnitude of the hit is a current hypothetical cause of the Younger Dryas Boundary Event. In a prior chapter we discussed how an event such as this killed off early North American human occupants &

megafauna and caused disastrous flooding across the northern hemisphere of the continent. The impact of the strike would have caused tsunamis across the North Atlantic and down into the South Atlantic. Further, if the meteor had broken into multiple pieces with some striking the ocean, or if the strike in Greenland produced a large amount of ice & rock ejecta; giant tsunamis could have been caused from this ejecta hitting the ocean. Large coastal areas could have been destroyed, changing the coastline and even the interior topography.

There is also significant evidence that sea-level rose a great deal after 12,000 BCE. Examining the data. we find the ocean levels rose between 80 to 100 meters covering costal areas and whatever there was of ancient human occupation.

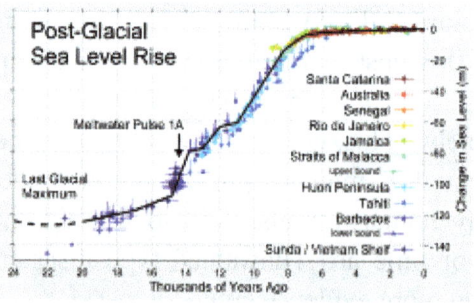

This conceivably would be significant in artifactual evidence being missing. An example of sea-level changes can be illustrated by looking at the semi-familiar New York City area. Below is a map of NYC with the current sea-level showing rivers, harbors and the majority of the population along the coast. It's estimated that 50 million people live within the Washington-Boston Northeast megalopolis, 30 miles from the coast. Prior to the

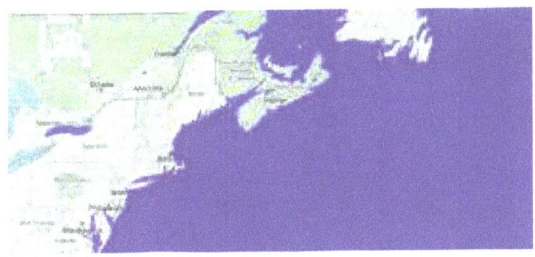

YDB Event the sea-level was 80 meters (262 feet) below the present level. The map below shows the amount of land area that was exposed during this time with present day NYC being 120 miles (193 kilometers) from the coast.

Viewing Google maps of the region we can certainly see the amount of area that was covered by water and the extension of the Hudson River coming out of New York City's Lower Bay. One of

the maps of the area is filtered and traces the Hudson River riverbed across the continental shelf in yellow. When we compare present day population centers, even with numerous interconnected superhighways and rapid transit systems, people still live within 30 miles of the

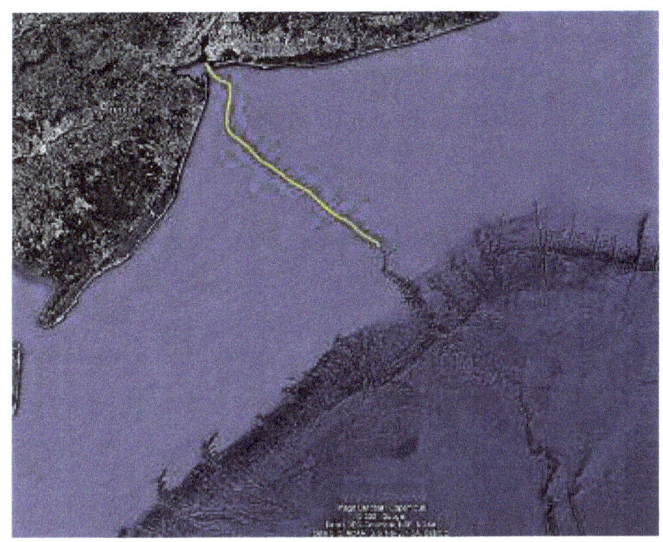

coast. Archaeologist examining this time period are limited in the area to investigate with much of it either underwater or nowhere near where advanced population areas were located.

This can be illustrated by raising the present day sea-level 80 meters (262 feet), the same amount

as after the YDB Event. Noticing the map above. all of NYC would be gone. Boston, Philadelphia, Baltimore, Washington DC, Long Island and all of New Jersey would cease to exist. Add 12,000 years and a destructive catastrophe that affected shorelines and inland topography, what would be left? Would archaeologists in the future be determining how technologically advanced and interconnected NYC was by excavating what was left of Allentown, Pennsylvania or Boston intricacies by excavating Worcester? Conceivably this is what we are doing when we examine pre-history sites. Investigation is of sparsely populated hills and not the urban population centers.

Nevertheless, I do think there is more than enough support pointing to Atlantis being a real place. Plato (429-347 BCE) and other later writers such as Cranto (335-275 BCE) and Plutarch (45-125 CE) held Atlantis as a real place. The map of Herodotus 450 BCE placed Atlantis (an oasis during his time) at the Richat Structure.

It seems Atlantis was a port city, beyond the Pillars of Hercules, on a now dry inland sea that had natural harbors, was fed by mountain streams and rivers and was accessible from the Ocean. Did the area look like the map below? How much do we need to shift out vision of the past?

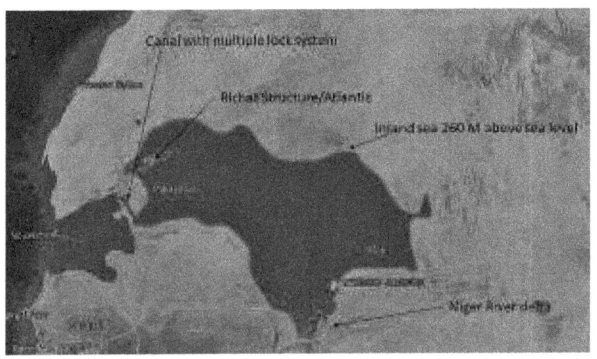

Studying a map of the Sahara Desert especially, of the El Djouf and Akchar deserts, we observe a number of geological and geographical phenomena. First, we find a river delta in the middle of the Niger

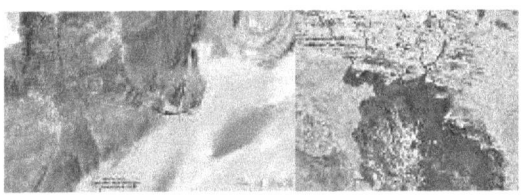

River system near Dialloubé, Mali. Deltas are typically found at the mouths of rivers entering into lakes, seas, oceans, and at times when flowing into the shallows of a slower moving river. This delta near Dialloubé seems to be a result of topographical change causing the Niger River to flow back into a single river and finding an alternate route.

Second, looking at the surrounding higher topography there are remnants of small mountain rivers and creeks; along with the Niger River entering into a large area known as the Taoudeni Basin.

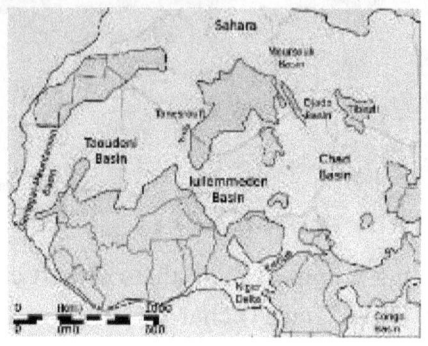

Taoudeni Basin is a Proterozoic era basin that contains 6,000 meters (20,000 feet) of Precambrian and Paleozoic sedimentary rock. Currently, there is between 21-43 meters (69-141 feet) of sand covering the sedimentary rock.[35] Because of planetary climate changes and a world-wide catastrophe, the planet's landscape was altered. Tsunamis, earthquakes and shifts in river courses caused some areas to be changed beyond recognition.

The Atlanteans may have had a large merchant fleet and navy of wooden ships. These ships could have had copper sheathed bottoms and similar to the 15th Century Ming Fleet commanded by Zheng He. His large fleet consisted of 317 ships, the

largest being the enormous treasure ships which were nine-masted, and about 127 meters (417 feet) long, 52 meters (171 feet) wide, with four decks and carrying up to 1000 people. He's voyages reached

from Africa and Arabia and across the Indian Ocean. Zheng He contacted the Asian sub-continent, and sailed the South China Sea, Philippine Sea and the Eastern Pacific. Some scholars believe one of the expeditions may have reached the Pacific coast of South America.[36]

If an Atlantean civilization existed, its reach would have been world-wide with various colonies and port trading cities. Could these colonies have included the Harappan society of the Indus Valley, ancient pre-dynastic Egypt, the Greek peninsula, or regions in South and Central America? Could there be ports that have been wiped out by tsunamis and earthquakes that are now hundreds of feet below the current ocean level? Then after adding on 12,000 years or more of time, would anything be found?

Structures would have been built out of stone and wood with building sophistication happening over time. Megalithic structures would have been used when necessary and balanced with delicate designs. Plato mentions that the buildings of Atlantis were built out of multi-colored stones of white, black and red. Some of the structures were simple and refined, while others were more ostentatious. One could imagine buildings with central heating, running water and indoor plumbing much as we would find in Rome thousands of years later.

Atlantean technology would have been based on basic physics, paradigm shifting metallurgy and the use of nature (windmills, waterwheels), steam, and mechanical manipulation (various four-bar linkages, cams, gearing) which used may have seemed almost magical.

We can imagine the Atlantean civilization as part of as a world-wide culture. Since we are dealing with modern humans then we would see the culture plagued with all the vicissitudes of humanity. We would find those who were prosperous, the merchant class, the poor and those who ruled over all the others politically and/or spiritually. As with today, or a thousand years ago, the period was marked with various power-centers with boundaries, capitals, and a way of defense. The typical human frailties of power struggles, war, impoverishment, and greed would be at work then as they are today.

Then one day, conceivably foreseen by early astronomers, it was gone. All of it destroyed by a disaster so great that it seems erased from human memory. An asteroid or comet with multiple fragments, entered the atmosphere and struck with such force that it caused earthquakes, tsunamis, and floods.

Along with the possibility of tidal waves speeding across the Atlantic, fragments and ejecta, possibly of ice, could have struck across the North and Mid-Atlantic Ocean. If a large piece or multiple pieces of ice were ejected and hit in an area such as Arguin Canyon or possibly in or around the Dakar or Kayor canyons off the coast of Mauritania the impact would have caused the ocean to wash over low-lying areas. This would have wiped clean any trace of buildings, and roads, resulting in the scrubbing of the countryside clean. Then add over

12 millennium and what would be found, what would still exist?

The final result was the rearranging of the coastline, the devastation of the interior portions of land, and the vaporization of glaciers and bedrock. This release of large amounts of water, rose the sea levels, and changed the world's ocean currents. The planet was struck and just like that a civilization was destroyed. The annihilation was not just of population centers of elegantly made cities, or those settlements in the hinter lands. It caused the extinction of entire herds and in some cases species of animals. The destroyed landscape was covered over with 100 feet of water and 12,000 years.

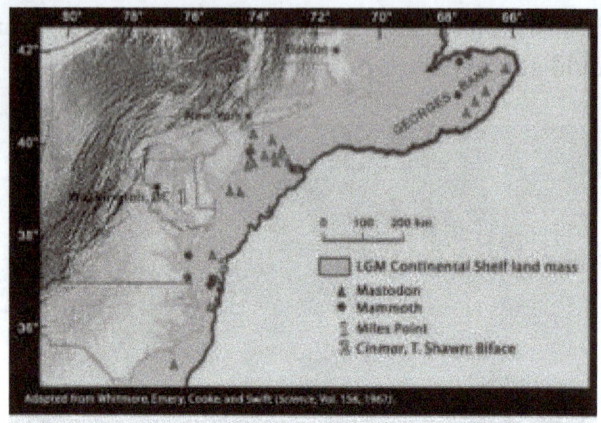

Map of the occurrence of Mastodon and Mammoth remains on the Continental Shelf.

"But afterward there occurred violent earthquakes and floods, and in a single day and night of rain all your warlike men in a body sunk into the earth, and the island of Atlantis in like manner disappeared, and was sunk beneath the sea."[37]

Appendix I
Plato's Atlantis Writings 360 BCE

Discourse of "Critias:" reprinted from "The Antediluvian World" by Ignatius Donnelly

Critias: Then listen, Socrates, to a strange tale, which is, however, certainly true, as Solon, who was the wisest of the seven sages, declared. He was a relative and great friend of my great-grandfather, Dropidas, as he himself says in several of his poems; and Dropidas told Critias, my grandfather, who remembered, and told us, that there were of old great and marvelous actions of the Athenians, which have passed into oblivion through time and the destruction of the human race and one in particular, which was the greatest of them all, the recital of which will be a suitable testimony of our gratitude to you....

Socrates: Very good; and what is this ancient famous action of which Critias spoke, not as a mere legend, but as a veritable action of the Athenian State, which Solon recounted!

Critias: I will tell an old-world story which I heard from an aged man; for Critias (the elder) was, as he said, at that time nearly ninety years of age, and I was about ten years of age. Now the day was that day of the Apaturia which is called the registration of youth; at which, according to custom, our parents gave prizes for recitations, and the poems of several poets were recited by us boys, and many of us sung the poems of Solon, which were new at the time.

One of our tribe, either because this was his real opinion, or because he thought that he would please Critias, said that, in his judgment, Solon was not only the wisest of men but the noblest of poets.

The old man, I well remember, brightened up at this, and said, smiling: "Yes, Amynander, if Solon had only, like other poets, made poetry the business of his life, and had completed the tale which he brought with him from Egypt, and had not been compelled, by reason of the factions and troubles which he found stirring in this country when he came home, to attend to other matters, in my opinion he would have been as famous as Homer, or Hesiod, or any poet."

"And what was that poem about, Critias?" said the person who addressed him.

"About the greatest action which the Athenians ever did, and which ought to have been most famous, but which, through the lapse of time and the destruction of the actors, has not come down to us."

"Tell us," said the other, "the whole story, and how and from whom Solon heard this veritable tradition."

He replied: "At the head of the Egyptian Delta, where the river Nile divides, there is a certain district which is called the district of Sais, and the great city of the district is also called Sais, and is the city from which Amasis the king was sprung. And the citizens have a deity who is their foundress: she is called in the Egyptian tongue Neith, which is asserted by them to be the same whom the Hellenes called Athene (Athena).

Now, the citizens of this city are great lovers of the Athenians and say that they are in some way related to them. Thither came Solon, who was received by them with great honor; and he asked the priests, who were most skillful in such matters, about antiquity, and made the discovery that neither he nor any other Hellene knew anything worth mentioning about the times of old.

On one occasion, when he was drawing them on to speak of antiquity, he began to tell about the most ancient things in our part of the world--about Phoroneus, who is called 'the first,' and about Niobe; and, after the Deluge, to tell of the lives of Deucalion and Pyrrha; and he traced the genealogy of their descendants, and attempted to reckon how many years old were the events of which he was speaking, and to give the dates.

Thereupon, one of the priests, who was of very great age; said, 'O Solon, Solon, you Hellenes are but children, and there is never an old man who is a Hellene.'

Solon, hearing this, said, 'What do you mean?'

'I mean to say,' he replied, 'that in mind you are all young; there is no old opinion handed down among you by ancient tradition, nor any science which is hoary with age. And I will tell you the reason of this: there have been, and there will be again, many destructions of mankind arising out of many causes.

There is a story which even you have preserved, that once upon a time Phaethon, the son of Helios, having yoked the steeds in his father's chariot, because he was not able to drive them in the path of his father, burnt up all that was upon the earth, and was himself destroyed by a thunderbolt. Now, this has the form of a myth, but really signifies a declination of the bodies moving around the earth and in the heavens, and a great conflagration of things upon the earth recurring at long intervals of time: when this happens, those who live upon the mountains and in dry and lofty places are more liable to destruction than those who dwell by rivers or on the sea-shore; and from this calamity the Nile, who is our never-failing savior, saves and delivers us.

When, on the other hand, the gods purge the earth with a deluge of water, among you herdsmen and shepherds on the mountains are the survivors, whereas those of you who live in cities are carried by the rivers into the sea; but in this country neither at that time nor at any other does the water come from above on the fields, having always a tendency to come up from below, for which reason the things preserved here are said to be the oldest.

The fact is, that wherever the extremity of winter frost or of summer sun does not prevent, the human race is always increasing at times, and at other times diminishing in numbers. And whatever happened either in your country or in ours, or in any other region of which we are informed--if any action which is noble or great, or in any other way remarkable has taken place, all that has been written down of old, and is preserved in our temples; whereas you and other nations are just being provided with letters and the other things which States require; and then, at the usual period, the stream from heaven descends like a pestilence, and leaves only those of you who are destitute of letters and education; and thus you have to begin all over again as children, and know nothing of what happened in ancient times, either among us or among yourselves.

As for those genealogies of yours which you have recounted to us, Solon, they are no better than the tales of children; for, in the first place, you remember one deluge only, whereas there were many of them; and, in the next place, you do not know that there dwelt in your land the fairest and noblest race of men which ever lived, of whom you and your whole city are but a seed or remnant. And this was unknown to you, because for many generations the survivors of that destruction died and made no sign.

For there was a time, Solon, before that great deluge of all, when the city which now is Athens was first in war, and was preeminent for the excellence of her laws, and is said to have performed the noblest deeds, and to have had the fairest constitution of any of which tradition tells, under the face of heaven.'

Solon marveled at this, and earnestly requested the priest to inform him exactly and in order about these former citizens.

'You are welcome to hear about them, Solon,' said the priest, 'both for your own sake and for that of the city; and, above all, for the sake of the goddess who is the common patron and protector and educator of both our cities. She founded your city a thousand years before ours, receiving from the Earth and Hephaestus the seed of your race, and then she founded ours, the constitution of which is set down in our sacred registers as 8000 years old.

As touching the citizens of 9000 years ago, I will briefly inform you of their laws and of the noblest of their actions; and the exact particulars of the whole we will hereafter go through at our leisure in the sacred registers themselves. If you compare these very laws with your own, you will find that many of ours are the counterpart of yours, as they were in the olden time.

In the first place, there is the caste of priests, which is separated from all the others; next there are the artificers, who exercise their several crafts by themselves, and without admixture of any other; and also there is the class of shepherds and that of hunters, as well as that of husbandmen; and you will observe, too, that the warriors in Egypt are separated from all the other classes, and are commanded by the law only to engage in war; moreover, the weapons with which they are equipped are shields and spears, and this the goddess taught first among you, and then in Asiatic countries, and we among the Asiatics first adopted.

"'Then, as to wisdom, do you observe what care the law took from the very first, searching out and comprehending the whole order of things down to prophecy and medicine, the latter with a view to health; and out of these divine elements drawing what was needful for human life, and adding every sort of knowledge which was connected with them.

All this order and arrangement the goddess first imparted to you when establishing your city; and she chose the spot of earth in which you were born, because she saw that the happy temperament of the seasons in that land would produce the wisest of men. Wherefore the goddess, who was a lover both of war and of wisdom, selected, and first of all settled that spot which was the most likely to produce men likest herself. And there you dwelt, having such laws as these and still better ones, and excelled all mankind in all virtue, as became the children and disciples of the gods.

Many great and wonderful deeds are recorded of your State in our histories; but one of them exceeds all the rest in greatness and valor; for these histories tell of a mighty power which was aggressing wantonly against the whole of Europe and Asia, and to which your city put an end.

This power came forth out of the Atlantic Ocean, for in those days the Atlantic was navigable; and there was an island situated in front of the straits which you call the Columns of Heracles (the Strait of Gibraltar, known as the Pillars of Hercules): the island was larger than Libya and Asia (Turkey) put together, and was the way to other islands, and from the islands you might pass through the whole of the opposite continent which surrounded the true ocean; for this sea which is within the Straits of Heracles is only a harbor, having a narrow entrance, but that other is a real sea, and the surrounding land may be most truly called a continent.

Now, in the island of Atlantis there was a great and wonderful empire, which had rule over the whole island and several others, as well as over parts of the continent; and, besides these, they subjected the parts of Libya within the Columns of Heracles as far as Egypt, and of Europe as far as Tyrrhenia (Italy).

The vast power thus gathered into one, endeavored to subdue at one blow our country and yours, and the whole of the land which was within the straits; and then, Solon, your country shone forth, in the excellence of her virtue and strength, among all mankind; for she was the first in courage and military skill, and was the leader of the Hellenes.

And when the rest fell off from her, being compelled to stand alone, after having undergone the very extremity of danger, she defeated and triumphed over the invaders, and preserved from slavery those who were not yet subjected, and freely liberated all the others who dwelt within the limits of Heracles.

But afterward there occurred violent earthquakes and floods, and in a single day and night of rain all your warlike men in a body sunk into the earth, and the island of Atlantis in like manner disappeared, and was sunk beneath the sea.

And that is the reason why the sea in those parts is impassable and impenetrable, because there is such a quantity of shallow mud in the way; and this was caused by the subsidence of the island.'[end excerpt.

Excerpt from "Timaeus" reprinted from "The Antediluvian World" by Ignatius Donnelly"

But in addition to the gods whom you have mentioned, I would specially invoke Mnemosyne; for all the important part of what I have to tell is dependent on her favor, and if I can recollect and recite enough of what was said by the priests, and brought hither by Solon, I doubt not that I shall satisfy the requirements of this theatre. To that task, then, I will at once address myself.

"Let me begin by observing, first of all, that nine thousand was the sum of years which had elapsed since the war which was said to have taken place between all those who dwelt outside the Pillars of Heracles and those who dwelt within them: this war I am now to describe.

Of the combatants on the one side the city of Athens was reported to have been the ruler, and to have directed the contest; the combatants on the other side were led by the kings of the islands of Atlantis, which, as I was saying, once had an extent greater than that of Libya and Asia (Turkey); and, when afterward sunk by an earthquake, became an impassable barrier of mud to voyagers sailing from hence to the ocean.

The progress of the history will unfold the various tribes of barbarians and Hellenes which then existed, as they successively appear on the scene; but I must begin by describing, first of all, the Athenians as they were in that day, and their enemies who fought with them; and I shall have to tell of the power and form of government of both of them. Let us give the precedence to Athens. . . (omitted?)

"Many great deluges have taken place during the nine thousand years, for that is the number of years which have elapsed since the time of which I am speaking; and in all the ages and changes of things there has never been any sediment of the earth flowing down from the mountains, as in other places, which is worth speaking of.

It has always been carried round in a circle and disappeared in the depths below. The consequence is that, in comparison of what then was, there are remaining in small islets only the bones of the wasted body, as they may be called, all the richer and softer parts of the soil having fallen away, and the mere skeleton of the country being left. . . .

"And next, if I have not forgotten what I heard when I was a child, I will impart to you the character and origin of their adversaries (the Atlanteans); for friends should not keep their stories to themselves, but have them in common. Yet, before proceeding farther in the narrative, I ought to warn you that you must not be surprised if you should hear Hellenic names given to foreigners.

I will tell you the reason of this: Solon, who was intending to use the tale for his poem, made an investigation into the meaning of the names, and found that the early Egyptians, in writing them down, had translated them into their own language, and he recovered the meaning of the several names and retranslated them, and copied them out again in our language. My great-grandfather, Dropidas, had the original writing, which is still in my possession, and was carefully studied by me when I was a child. Therefore, if you hear names such as are used in this country, you must not be surprised, for I have told you the reason of them.

"The tale, which was of great length, began as follows: I have before remarked, in speaking of the allotments of the gods, that they distributed the whole earth into portions differing in extent, and made themselves temples and sacrifices. And Poseidon, receiving for his lot the island of Atlantis, begat children by a mortal woman, and settled them in a part of the island which I will proceed to describe.

On the side toward the sea, and in the center of the whole island, there was a plain which is said to have been the fairest of all plains, and very fertile. Near the plain again, and also in the center of the island, at a distance of about fifty stadia (one stadia=606 feet), there was a mountain, not very high on any side.

In this mountain there dwelt one of the earth-born primeval men of that country, whose name was Evenor, and he had a wife named Leucippe, and they had an only daughter, who was named Cleito. The maiden was growing up to womanhood when her father and mother died.

Poseidon fell in love with her, and had intercourse with her; and, breaking the ground, enclosed the hill in which she dwelt all round, making alternate zones of sea and land, larger and smaller, encircling one another; there were two of land and three of water, which he turned as with a lathe out of the center of the island, equidistant every way, so that no man could get to the island, for ships and voyages were not yet heard of.

He himself, as he was a god, found no difficulty in making special arrangements for the center island, bringing two streams of water under the earth, which he caused to ascend as springs, one of warm water and the other of cold, and making every variety of food to spring up abundantly in the earth.

He also begat and brought up five pairs of male children, dividing the island of Atlantis into ten portions: he gave to the first-born of the eldest pair his mother's dwelling and the surrounding allotment, which was the largest and best, and made him king over the rest; the others he made princes, and gave them rule over many men and a large territory.

And he named them all: the eldest, who was king, he named Atlas, and from him the whole island and the ocean received the name of Atlantic. To his twin-brother, who was born after him, and obtained as his lot the extremity of the island toward the Pillars of Heracles, as far as the country which is still called the region of Gades in that part of the world, he gave the name which in the Hellenic language is Eumelus, in the language of the country which is named after him, Gadeirus.

Of the second pair of twins, he called one Ampheres and the other Evaemon. To the third pair of twins he gave the name Mneseus to the elder, and Autochthon to the one who followed him. Of the fourth pair of twins he called the elder Elasippus and the younger Mestor, And of the fifth pair be gave to the elder the name of Azaes, and to the younger Diaprepes.

All these and their descendants were the inhabitants and rulers of divers islands in the open sea; and also, as has been already said, they held sway in the other direction over the country within the Pillars as far as Egypt and Tyrrhenia (Italy).

Now Atlas had a numerous and honorable family, and his eldest branch always retained the kingdom, which the eldest son handed on to his eldest for many generations; and they had such an amount of wealth as was never before possessed by kings and potentates, and is not likely ever to be again, and they were furnished with everything which they could have, both in city and country. For, because of the greatness of their empire, many things were brought to them from foreign countries, and the island itself provided much of what was required by them for the uses of life.

In the first place, they dug out of the earth whatever was to be found there, mineral as well as metal, and that which is now only a name, and was then something more than a name -- orichalcum -- was dug out of the earth in many parts of the island, and, with the exception of gold, was esteemed the most precious of metals among the men of those days.

There was an abundance of wood for carpenters' work, and sufficient maintenance for tame and wild animals. Moreover, there were a great number of elephants in the island, and there was provision for animals of every kind, both for those which live in lakes and marshes and rivers, and also for those which live in mountains and on plains, and therefore for the animal which is the largest and most voracious of them.

Also, whatever fragrant things there are in the earth, whether roots, or herbage, or woods, or distilling drops of flowers or fruits, grew and thrived in that land; and again, the cultivated fruit of the earth, both the dry edible fruit and other species of food, which we call by the general name of legumes, and the fruits having a hard rind, affording drinks, and meats, and ointments, and good store of chestnuts and the like, which may be used to play with, and are fruits which spoil with keeping--and the pleasant kinds of dessert which console us after dinner, when we are full and tired of eating--all these that sacred island lying beneath the sun brought forth fair and wondrous in infinite abundance.

All these things they received from the earth, and they employed themselves in constructing their temples, and palaces, and harbors, and docks; and they arranged the whole country in the following manner: First of all they bridged over the zones of sea which surrounded the ancient metropolis, and made a passage into and out of the royal palace; they began to build the palace and then the habitation of the god and of their ancestors. This they continued to ornament in successive generations, every king surpassing the one who came before him to the utmost of his power, until they made the building a marvel to behold for size and for beauty.

And, beginning from the sea, they dug a canal three hundred feet in width and one hundred feet in depth, and fifty stadia in length, which they carried through to the outermost zone, making a passage from the sea up to this, which became a harbor, and leaving an opening sufficient to enable the largest vessels to find ingress. Moreover, they divided the zones of land which parted the zones of sea, constructing bridges of such a width as would leave a passage for a single trireme to pass out of one into another, and roofed them over; and there was a way underneath for the ships, for the banks of the zones were raised considerably above the water.

Now the largest of the zones into which a passage was cut from the sea was three stadia in breadth, and the zone of land which came next of equal breadth; but the next two, as well the zone of water as of land, were two stadia, and the one which surrounded the central island was a stadium only in width. The island in which the palace was situated had a diameter of five stadia.

This, and the zones and the bridge, which was the sixth part of a stadium in width, they surrounded by a stone wall, on either side placing towers, and gates on the bridges where the sea passed in. The stone which was used in the work they quarried from underneath the center island and from underneath the zones, on the outer as well as the inner side. One kind of stone was white, another black, and a third red; and, as they quarried, they at the same time hollowed out docks double within, having roofs formed out of the native rock. Some of their buildings were simple, but in others they put together different stones, which they intermingled for the sake of ornament, to be a natural source of delight.

The entire circuit of the wall which went round the outermost one they covered with a coating of brass, and the circuit of the next wall they coated with tin, and the third, which encompassed the citadel flashed with the red light of orichalcum.

The palaces in the interior of the citadel were constructed in this wise: In the center was a holy temple dedicated to Cleito and Poseidon, which remained inaccessible, and was surrounded by an enclosure of gold; this was the spot in which they originally begat the race of the ten princes, and thither they annually brought the fruits of the earth in their season from all the ten portions, and performed sacrifices to each of them. Here, too, was Poseidon's own temple, of a stadium in length and half a stadium in width, and of a proportionate height, having a sort of barbaric splendor.

All the outside of the temple, with the exception of the pinnacles, they covered with silver, and the pinnacles with gold. In the interior of the temple the roof was of ivory, adorned everywhere with gold and silver and orichalcum; all the other parts of the walls and pillars and floor they lined with orichalcum. In the temple they placed statues of gold: there was the god himself standing in a chariot--the charioteer of six winged horses--and of such a size that he touched the roof of the building with his head; around him there were a hundred Nereids riding on dolphins, for such was thought to be the number of them in that day.

There were also in the interior of the temple other images which had been dedicated by private individuals. And around the temple on the outside were placed statues of gold of all the ten kings and of their wives; and there were many other great offerings, both of kings and of private individuals, coming both from the city itself and the foreign cities over which they held sway. There was an altar, too, which in size and workmanship corresponded to the rest of the work, and there were palaces in like manner which answered to the greatness of the kingdom and the glory of the temple.

"In the next place, they used fountains both of cold and hot springs; these were very abundant, and both kinds wonderfully adapted to use by reason of the sweetness and excellence of their waters. They constructed buildings about them, and planted suitable trees; also cisterns, some open to the heaven, other which they roofed over, to be used in winter as warm baths, there were the king's baths, and the baths of private persons, which were kept apart; also separate baths for women, and others again for horses and cattle, and to them they gave as much adornment as was suitable for them.

The water which ran off they carried, some to the grove of Poseidon, where were growing all manner of trees of wonderful height and beauty, owing to the excellence of the soil; the remainder was conveyed by aqueducts which passed over the bridges to the outer circles: and there were many temples built and dedicated to many gods; also gardens and places of exercise, some for men, and some set apart for horses, in both of the two islands formed by the zones; and in the center of the larger of the two there was a race-course of a stadium in width, and in length allowed to extend all-round the island, for horses to race in.

Also there were guard-houses at intervals for the body-guard, the more trusted of whom had their duties appointed to them in the lesser zone, which was nearer the Acropolis; while the most trusted of all had houses given them within the citadel, and about the persons of the kings. The docks were full of triremes and naval stores, and all things were quite ready for use.

Enough of the plan of the royal palace. Crossing the outer harbors, which were three in number, you would come to a wall which began at the sea and went all round: this was everywhere distant fifty stadia from the largest zone and harbor, and enclosed the whole, meeting at the mouth of the channel toward the sea. The entire area was densely crowded with habitations; and the canal and the largest of the harbors were full of vessels and merchants coming from all parts, who, from their numbers, kept up a multitudinous sound of human voices and din of all sorts night and day.

I have repeated his descriptions of the city and the parts about the ancient palace nearly as he gave them, and now I must endeavor to describe the nature and arrangement of the rest of the country. The whole country was described as being very lofty and precipitous on the side of the sea, but the country immediately about and surrounding the city was a level plain, itself surrounded by mountains which descended toward the sea; it was smooth and even, but of an oblong shape, extending in one direction three thousand stadia, and going up the country from the sea through the center of the island two thousand stadia; the whole region of the island lies toward the south, and is sheltered from the north.

The surrounding mountains he celebrated for their number and size and beauty, in which they exceeded all that are now to be seen anywhere; having in them also many wealthy inhabited villages, and rivers and lakes, and meadows supplying food enough for every animal, wild or tame, and wood of various sorts, abundant for every kind of work.

I will now describe the plain, which had been cultivated during many ages by many generations of kings. It was rectangular, and for the most part straight and oblong; and what it wanted of the straight line followed the line of the circular ditch.

The depth and width and length of this ditch were incredible and gave the impression that such a work, in addition to so many other works, could hardly have been wrought by the hand of man. But I must say what I have heard. It was excavated to the depth of a hundred feet, and its breadth was a stadium everywhere; it was carried round the whole of the plain and was ten thousand stadia in length.

It received the streams which came down from the mountains, and winding round the plain, and touching the city at various points, was there let off into the sea. From above, likewise, straight canals of a hundred feet in width were cut in the plain, and again let off into the ditch, toward the sea; these canals were at intervals of a hundred stadia, and by them they brought down the wood from the mountains to the city, and conveyed the fruits of the earth in ships, cutting transverse passages from one canal into another, and to the city.

Twice in the year they gathered the fruits of the earth--in winter having the benefit of the rains, and in summer introducing the water of the canals. As to the population, each of the lots in the plain had an appointed chief of men who were fit for military service, and the size of the lot was to be a square of ten stadia each way, and the total number of all the lots was sixty thousand.

"And of the inhabitants of the mountains and of the rest of the country there was also a vast multitude having leaders, to whom they were assigned according to their dwellings and villages. The leader was required to furnish for the war the sixth portion of a war-chariot, so as to make up a total of ten thousand chariots; also two horses and riders upon them, and a light chariot without a seat, accompanied by a fighting man on foot carrying a small shield, and having a charioteer mounted to guide the horses; also, he was bound to furnish two heavy-armed men, two archers, two slingers, three stone-shooters, and three javelin men, who were skirmishers, and four sailors to make up a complement of twelve hundred ships.

Such was the order of war in the royal city--that of the other nine governments was different in each of them and would be wearisome to narrate. As to offices and honors, the following was the arrangement from the first: Each of the ten kings, in his own division and in his own city, had the absolute control of the citizens, and in many cases of the laws, punishing and slaying whomsoever he would.

"Now the relations of their governments to one another were regulated by the injunctions of Poseidon as the law had handed them down. These were inscribed by the first men on a column of orichalcum, which was situated in the middle of the island, at the temple of Poseidon, whither the people were gathered together every fifth and sixth years alternately, thus giving equal honor to the odd and to the even number.

And when they were gathered together, they consulted about public affairs, and inquired if anyone had transgressed in anything, and passed judgment on him accordingly--and before they passed judgment they gave their pledges to one another in this wise:

There were bulls who had the range of the temple of Poseidon; and the ten who were left alone in the temple, after they had offered prayers to the gods that they might take the sacrifices which were acceptable to them, hunted the bulls without weapons, but with staves and nooses; and the bull which they caught they led up to the column; the victim was then struck on the head by them, and slain over the sacred inscription.

Now on the column, besides the law, there was inscribed an oath invoking mighty curses on the disobedient. When, therefore, after offering sacrifice according to their customs, they had burnt the limbs of the bull, they mingled a cup and cast in a clot of blood for each of them; the rest of the victim they took to the fire, after having made a purification of the column all round.

Then they drew from the cup in golden vessels, and, pouring a libation on the fire, they swore that they would judge according to the laws on the column, and would punish anyone who had previously transgressed, and that for the future they would not, if they could help, transgress any of the inscriptions, and would not command or obey any ruler who commanded them to act otherwise than according to the laws of their father Poseidon.

This was the prayer which each of them offered up for himself and for his family, at the same time drinking, and dedicating the vessel in the temple of the god; and, after spending some necessary time at supper, when darkness came on and the fire about the sacrifice was cool, all of them put on most beautiful azure robes, and, sitting on the ground at night near the embers of the sacrifices on which they had sworn, and extinguishing all the fire about the temple, they received and gave judgment, if any of them had any accusation to bring against any one; and, when they had given judgment, at daybreak they wrote down their sentences on a golden tablet, and deposited them as memorials with their robes.

There were many special laws which the several kings had inscribed about the temples, but the most important was the following: That they were not to take up arms against one another, and they were all to come to the rescue if anyone in any city attempted to over throw the royal house. Like their ancestors, they were to deliberate in common about war and other matters, giving the supremacy to the family of Atlas; and the king was not to have the power of life and death over any of his kinsmen, unless he had the assent of the majority of the ten kings.

"Such was the vast power which the god settled in the lost island of Atlantis; and this he afterward directed against our land on the following pretext, as traditions tell: For many generations, as long as the divine nature lasted in them, they were obedient to the laws, and well-affectioned toward the gods, who were their kinsmen; for they possessed true and in every way great spirits, practicing gentleness and wisdom in the various chances of life, and in their intercourse with one another.

They despised everything but virtue, not caring for their present state of life, and thinking lightly on the possession of gold and other property, which seemed only a burden to them; neither were they intoxicated by luxury; nor did wealth deprive them of their self-control; but they were sober, and saw clearly that all these goods are increased by virtuous friendship with one another, and that by excessive zeal for them, and honor of them, the good of them is lost, and friendship perishes with them.

"By such reflections, and by the continuance in them of a divine nature, all that which we have described waxed and increased in them; but when this divine portion began to fade away in them, and became diluted too often, and with too much of the mortal admixture, and the human nature got the upper-hand, then, they being unable to bear their fortune, became unseemly.

To him who had an eye to see, they began to appear base, and had lost the fairest of their precious gifts; but to those who had no eye to see the true happiness, they still appeared glorious and blessed at the very time when they were filled with unrighteous avarice and power.

Zeus, the god of gods, who rules with law, and is able to see into such things, perceiving that an honorable race was in a most wretched state, and wanting to inflict punishment on them, that they might be chastened and improved, collected all the gods into his most holy habitation, which, being placed in the center of the world, sees all things that partake of generation. And when he had called them together, he spake as follows. . .

Appendix 2
Maps & Enlarged Photos

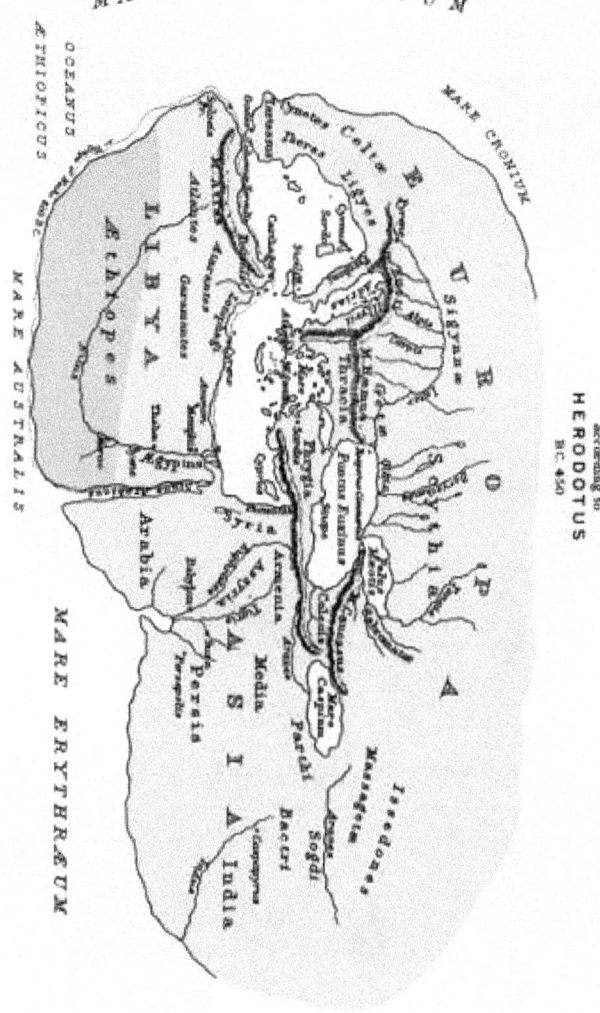

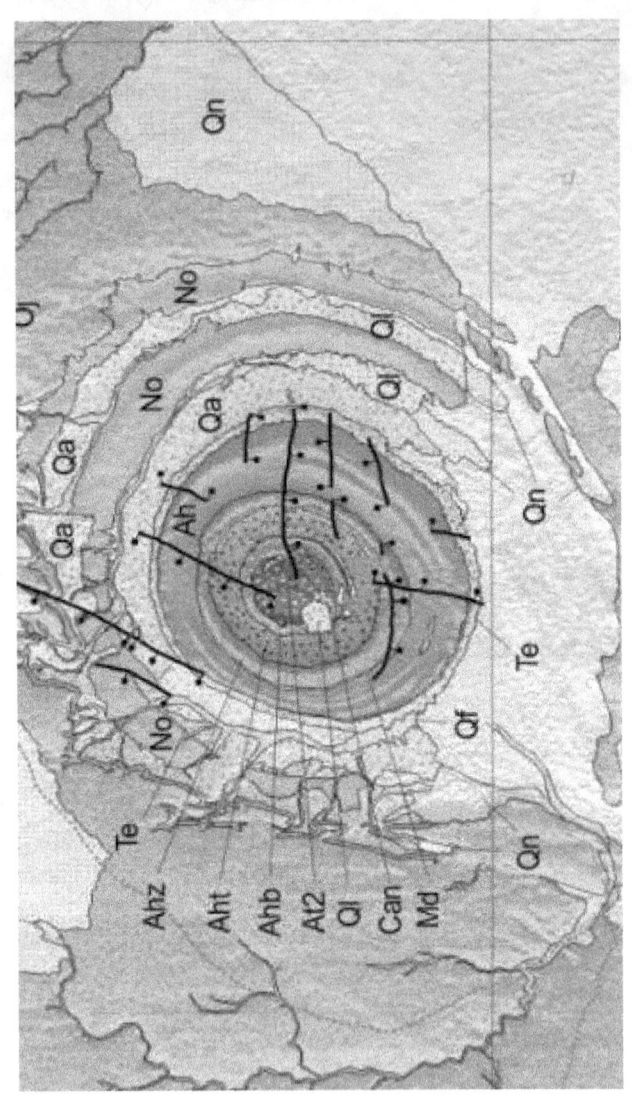

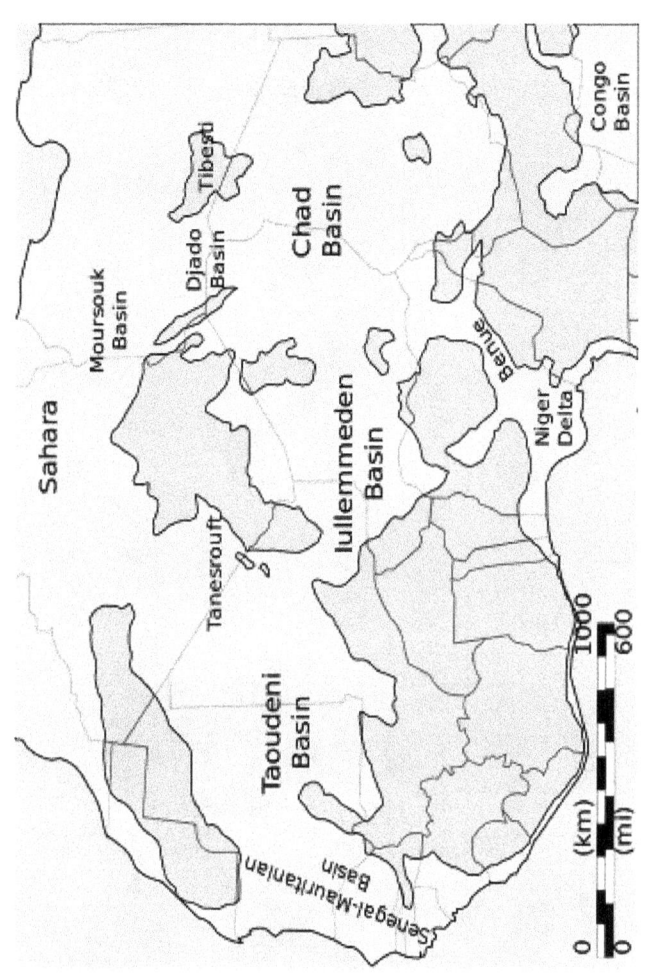

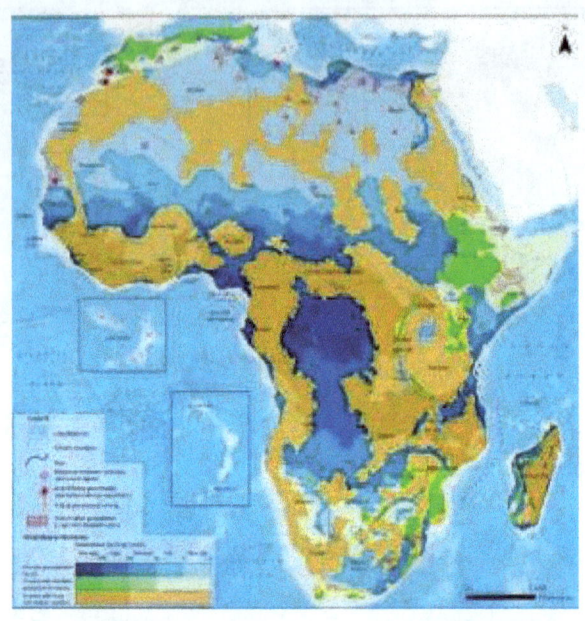

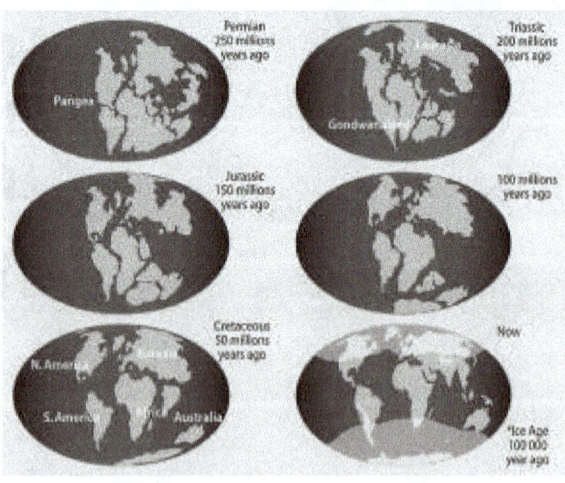

The Spread of Agriculture

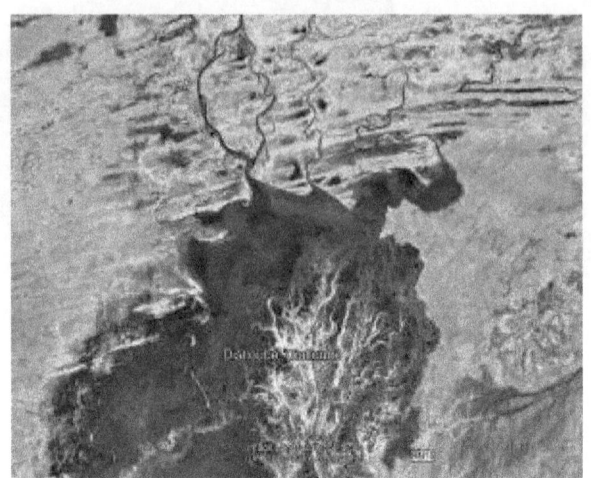

Niger River delta in desert

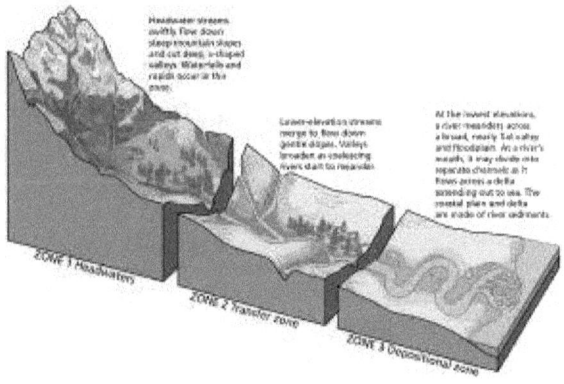

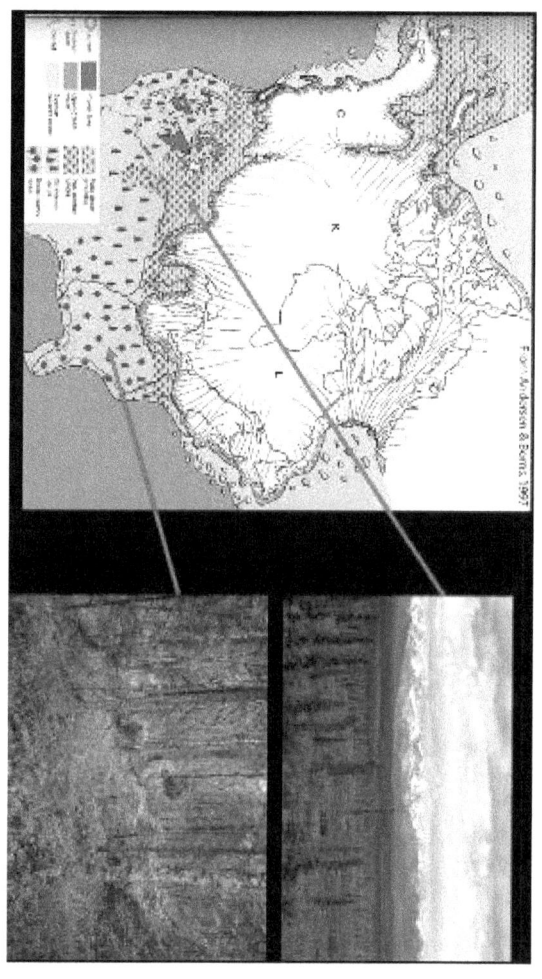

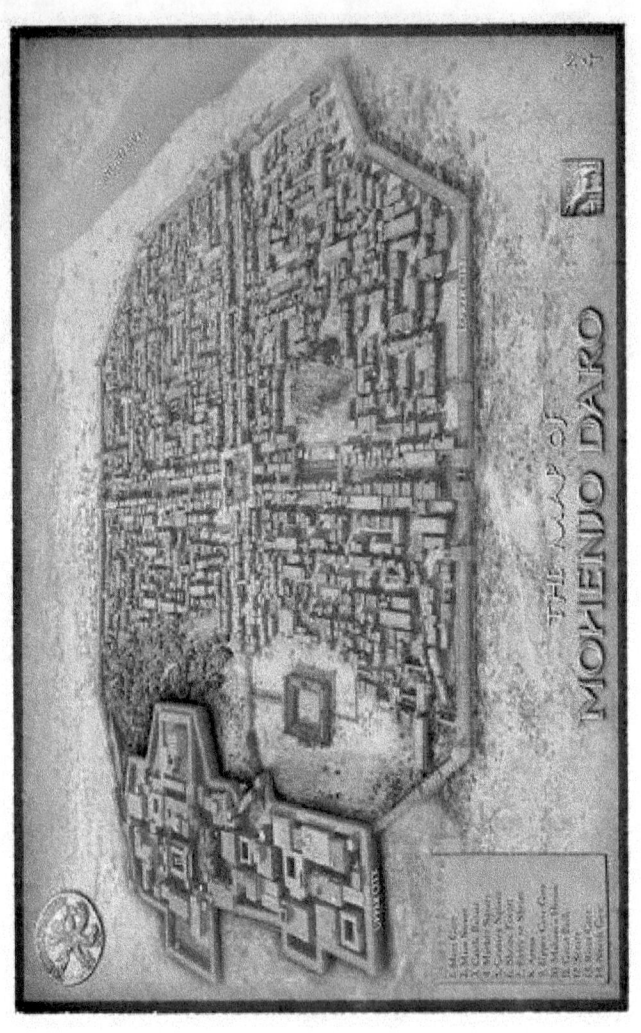

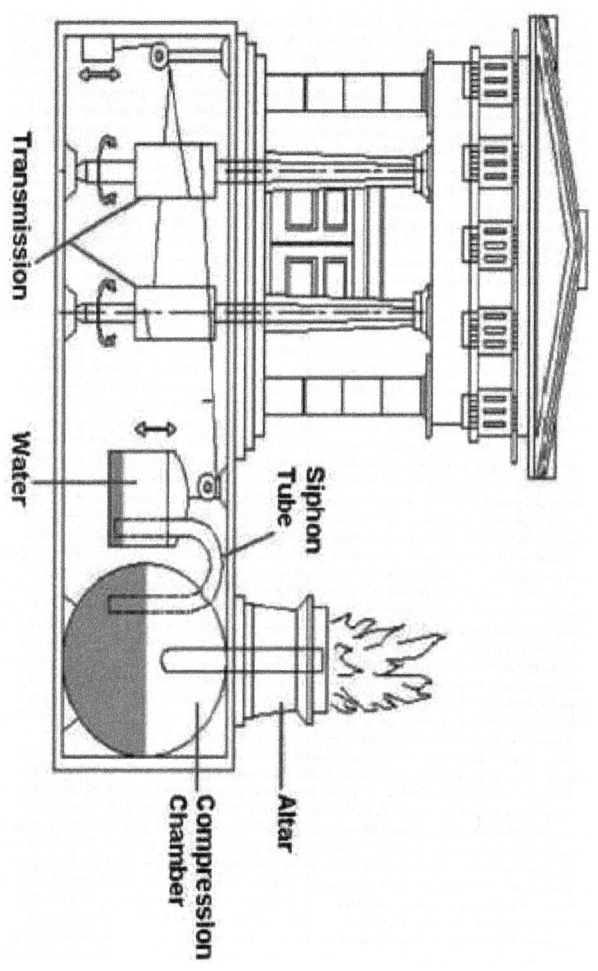

Drawing depicting the components of Heron's automatic door.
Aircompressorworks.com

Appendix 3
Further Resource Material

As I wrote earlier this book is a tertiary work, a collection of information, facts, and recent interpretations of history and archaeology found from other sources and combined with my interpretation of the material.

Included is a list of authors, works and other sources I've used or referred to in writing this book. I encourage the reader to investigate each of these researchers/authors/lecturers. Read over their research and writings. Many have podcasts or have been on podcasts and listen to what they have discovered and make your own conclusions. The suggestions include:

Randal Carlson

Randall Carlson, known as a master builder and architectural designer and recognized as a teacher, geometrician, geomythologist, geological explorer. To some he is just a renegade scholar. Carlson has over four decades of study, research and exploration into the interface between ancient mysteries and modern science. He has been recognized by The National Science Teachers Association for his commitment to Science education for young people.[38]

Suggested works and videos:
Kosmographia https://randallcarlson.comon
Kosmographia YouTube/ https://www.youtube.com/c/RandallCarlson1440/about
Joe Rogan Experience Podcast episodes: #606, #872, #961, & #1284.

Brien Foerster

Brien Foerster was raised on the west coast of Canada, and developed an interest, of the Native people, their art, and oral traditions. This led to his becoming a professional sculptor and graduated with an honors BSc degree from the University Of Victoria. In 1995 he moved to Maui, Hawaii, and was hired as assistant project manager for the building of the 62-foot double hull sailing canoe Mo'okiha O Pi'ilani and the restoration of the famous Mo'olele sailing canoe. He next went to Peru and studied Inca culture which led to his book, *A Brief History Of The Incas*. He is now the assistant director of the Paracas History Museum in Paracas, south of Lima. Other published books include information on the ancient history of Hawaii, and the mysterious stone monuments of Peru that predate the Inca. He is the author of 22 books.[39]

Suggested works and videos:
Hidden Inca Tours

https://hiddenincatours.com
Brien Foerster YouTube/
https://www.youtube.com/
channel/UCOavg1FtdeuyUTLz3wmuIKQ

Graham Hancock

Graham Hancock was born in Edinburgh, Scotland with his early years being spent in India, where his father was a surgeon. He went to school and university in the northern English city of Durham where he graduated from Durham University in 1973 with First Class Honors in Sociology. He pursued a career in journalism, writing for many of Britain's leading newspapers including The Times, The Sunday Times, The Independent, and The Guardian. He was co-editor of New Internationalist magazine from 1976-1979 and East Africa correspondent of The Economist from 1981-1983. In the early 1980's he began to move consistently in the direction of books.[40]

Suggested works and videos:

Graham Hancock https://grahamhancock.com
The Sign and the Seal: The Quest for the Lost Ark of the Covenant. New York: Crown.
Fingerprints of the Gods: The Evidence of Earth's Lost Civilization. New York: Crown Publishers.
The Message of the Sphinx: A Quest for the Hidden Legacy of Mankind. New York: Crown Publishers. Published in the United Kingdom as Hancock, Graham; Robert Bauval (1996). *Keeper of Genesis:*

A Quest for the Hidden Legacy of Mankind. London: Heinemann.
The Mars Mystery: A Tale of the End of Two Worlds. London: Michael Joseph.
Heaven's Mirror: Quest for the Lost Civilization. New York: Crown Publishers.
Fingerprints of the Gods: The Quest Continues (New Updated ed.). New York: Crown Century.
Underworld: The Mysterious Origins of Civilization. New York: Crown.
Talisman: Sacred Cities, Secret Faith. Tisbury: Element Books.
Supernatural: Meeting with the Ancient Teachers of Mankind. London: Century.
Entangled: The Eater of Souls. New York: The Disinformation Company.
War God: Nights of the Witch. Coronet.
Magicians of the Gods: The Forgotten Wisdom of Earth's Lost Civilization. Coronet
America Before: The Key to Earth's Lost Civilization. St. Martin's Press.
Michael Palin's Pole to Pole – Crossing the Line (EP 5) (1992)
Quest for the Lost Civilization – Acorn Media (1998)
Atlantis Reborn Again – BBC Horizon (2000)
Earth Pilgrims – Earth Pilgrims Inc. (2010)
"The War on Consciousness" – TEDx (2013)

Joe Rogan Experience, episodes #551, #725, #872, #961, #1284.

Charles C. Mann

Charles Mann was a correspondent for The Atlantic, Science, and Wired, and has also written for Fortune, The New York Times, Smithsonian, Technology Review, Vanity Fair, and The Washington Post, as well as for the TV network HBO and the series Law & Order. He is a three-time National Magazine Award finalist and is the recipient of writing awards from the American Bar Association, the American Institute of Physics, the Alfred P. Sloan Foundation, and the Lannan Foundation. His book 1491 won the National Academies Communication Award for the best book of the year.[41]

Suggested works and videos:
1491: New Revelations of the Americas Before Columbus, Knopf, 2005
"Our Good Earth: The future rests on the soil beneath our feet; Can we save it?" National Geographic, September 2008. 80–107.
"The Birth of Religion", National Geographic, June 2011. 34–59.
1493: Uncovering the New World Columbus Created, Knopf, 2011
"State of the Species: Does success spell doom for Homo sapiens?", Orion Magazine, November/December 2012.

1493 for Young People: From Columbus's Voyage to Globalization, Seven Stories Press, 2015.

Natalis Rosen and George S. Alexander, the film *Visiting Atlantis*.

George Alexander and Natalis Rosen have established a website[42] promoting the Richat Structure, in Mauritania, as the location of the city of Atlantis. They are not the first to make this suggestion but have at least visited the site in 2008 to gather evidence to support their contention. Their expedition formed the basis for a free one-hour video.[43] Like supporters of various other locations theories, Alexander and Rosen have managed to match some of the details in Plato's description with features in the Richat area. The Richat Structure is around 35 km in diameter yet no evidence whatsoever of buildings whatsoever was found.[44]

Suggested Works:
Website: *Visiting Atlantis*
https://visitingatlantis.com/

Robert Schoch

Dr. Robert M. Schoch, faculty member at the College of General Studies at Boston University since 1984. He earned his Ph.D. in Geology and Geophysics at Yale University in 1983 also holding an M.S. and M.Phil. in Geology and Geophysics from Yale, as well as degrees in Anthropology (B.A.) and Geology (B.S.) from George

Washington University. In 2017, the College of General Studies at Boston University named him Director of its Institute for the Study of the Origins of Civilization (ISOC). In the early 1990s, Dr. Schoch stunned the world with his revolutionary research that recast the date of the Great Sphinx of Egypt to a period thousands of years earlier than its standard attribution.[45]

Suggested works and videos:
Phylogeny Reconstruction in Paleontology, 1986.
Systematics, Functional Morphology and Macroevolution of the Extinct Mammalian Order Taeniodonta, 1986.
Stratigraphy: Principles and Methods, 1989.
Voices of the Rocks: A Scientist Looks at Catastrophes and Ancient Civilizations, 1999.
Horns, Tusks, and Flippers: The Evolution of Hoofed Mammals, with Donald R. Prothero, 2003.
Voyages of the Pyramid Builders: The True Origins of the Pyramids from Lost Egypt to Ancient America, 2003.
Environmental Science: Systems and Solutions, with Michael McKinney, 2003.
Pyramid Quest: Secrets of the Great Pyramid and the Dawn of Civilization, Tarcher Perigee, 2005.
Environmental Science: Systems and Solutions, with Michael L. Mcinney, Logan Yonavjak, 2007.
Forgotten Civilization, The Role of Solar Outbursts in Our Past and Future, 2012.

Origins of the Sphinx: Celestial Guardian of Pre-Pharaonic Civilization, with Robert Bauval, 2017.
Website: *The Official Website of Robert M. Schoch*, https://www.robertschoch.com/index.html

John Anthony West

John A. West is a prominent advocate of the Symbolist school of Egyptology and is an author, scholar, and Pythagorean. He is the author of *The Traveler's Key to Ancient Egypt* and consulting editor for the *Traveler's Key* series. West is an authority on Sphinx water erosion hypothesis in geology. He believes in the alternate understanding of ancient Egyptian culture in which architecture and art disclose a collective knowledge than what orthodox Egyptology assumes. In 1993 West's work with Robert M. Schoch, a geologist and associate professor at Boston University was in an NBC special called *The Mystery of the Sphinx*.

Suggested works and videos:
Serpent in the Sky: The High Wisdom of Ancient Egypt, Quest Books, 1993
The Traveler's Key to Ancient Egypt: A Guide to the Sacred Places of Ancient Egypt, Quest Books, 1996
The Science of the Dogon: Decoding the African Mystery Tradition, Quest Books, 2006
Sacred Symbols of the Dogon: The Key to Advanced Science in the Ancient Egyptian Hieroglyphs, Quest Books, 2007

Ancient Egypt Mystery Schools, Unusual Accomplishment, LLC., 2015
Magical Egypt: A Symbolist Tour of Ancient Egypt, 8 episodes, Cydonia Inc., 2001

Nick Zenter

Nick Zenter earned a BS in Geology from the University of Wisconsin and an MS in Geology from Idaho State University. He has taught in higher education since 1989 and since 1992 has taught at Central Washington University. In 2015, Nick received the esteemed James Shea Award, a national award acknowledging extraordinary delivery of Earth Science to the general public.[46]

Suggested works and videos:
Extension and Subsidence of the Eastern Snake River Plain, Idaho 2002
Nick On The Rocks: 2016-present/18 episodes, produced for KCTS (PBS-TV in Seattle, Washington.
Downtown Geology Lectures: 2010-present/26 lectures, produced by CWU in Ellensburg, Washington.
I-90 Rocks and other Special Topics: 2014-2015/6 episodes, by Hugefloods.com in Pasco, Washington.
2 Minute Geology: 2012-2014/17 episodes, produced by Hugefloods.com in Pasco, Washington.

Central Rocks - Roadside Geology: 2011-2012/8 episodes, produced by CWU in Ellensburg, Washington.

Central Rocks, Interviews with Geologists: 2005-2012/33 episodes produced by CWU in Ellensburg, Washington.

End Notes

[1] Stargate: Atlantis (TV Series 2004–2009), IMDb.
[2] Britannica, T. Editors of Encyclopaedia. "Quipu." Encyclopedia Britannica, April 6, 2016. https://www.britannica.com/technology/Quipu.
[3] The Smithsonian Institution's, *Australopithecus afarensis The Smithsonian Institution's Human Origins Program*, 2021, https://humanorigins.si.edu/evidence/human-fossils/species/australopithecus-afarensis.
[4] Williams, F. L'Engle , Trinkaus, . Erik and Tuttle, Russell Howard. "Neanderthal." Encyclopedia Britannica, February 6, 2020. https://www.britannica.com/topic/Neanderthal.
[5] Groeneveld, Emma. "Denisovan." World History Encyclopedia. Last modified March 05, 2019. https://www.ancient.eu/Denisovan/.
[6] Rafferty, J. P. "Homo sapiens." Encyclopedia Britannica, July 2, 2020. https://www.britannica.com/topic/Homo-sapiens-sapiens.
[7] All information and photos on Skare Brae are from *Orkneyjar - The Heritage of the Orkney Islands* website & is either a direct quote or paraphrase.
[8] Stephanie Dalley, *Myths from Mesopotamia*, (Oxford: Oxford University Press) 1989, 40–41
[9] Old Testament (Torah) Genesis 6:9-9:17

[10] NS Gill, *Atlantis as It Was Told in Plato's Socratic Dialogues*, Thoughtco, https://www.thoughtco.com/platos-atlantis-from-the-timaeus-119667, October 5, 2018.

[11] *Ibid.*

[12] *Ibid.*

[13] Muratori, *Chronicon Estense in Rerum Italicarum Scriptores*, 15, III. pp. 159-164 as cited by Phillip Ziegler, *The Black Death,* (New York: Harper Collins) 1969, 14.

[14] NOAA: National Centers for Environmental Information. *Perspectives Abrupt Climate Change: The Younger* Dryas, Department of Commerce: US Government, https://www.ncdc.noaa.gov/abrupt-climate-change/The%20Younger%20Dryas.

[15] *Ibid.*

[16] *Ibid.*

[17] Volker Dietrich, & Lagios, Gregor. (2019). 12,800 years ago, Hellas and the World on Fire and Flood. *Journal of Geography and earth Sciences.* 7. 10.15640/jges.v7n1a9.

[18] Brian Clark Howard, *City-size impact crater found under Greenland Ice. National Geographic* ttps://www.nationalgeographic.com/science/2018/11/impact-crater-found-under-hiawatha-glacier-greenland-ice/.

[19] Kathryn Ried, *2004 Indian Ocean earthquake and tsunami: Facts, FAQs, and how to help*, Federal Way, WA: World Vision, December 26, 2019 https://www.worldvision.org/disaster-relief-news-stories/2004-indian-ocean-earthquake-tsunami-facts

[20] Peter B. deMenocal & Jessica E. Tierney. *Green Sahara: African Humid Periods Paced by Earth's Orbital Changes*, (Cambridge, MA: Nature Education) https://www.nature.com/scitable/knowledge/library/green-sahara-african-humid-periods-paced-by-82884405/.
[21] *Ibid.*
[22] *Ibid.*
[23] *Ibid.*
[24] G.I. Alsop, R. Weinberger, T. Levi, S. Marco, *Cycles of passive versus active diapirism recorded along an exposed salt wall,* Journal of Structural Geology, Volume 84, 2016, Pages 47-67,
[25] Everett R. Holles, "Psychic Group to Seek Lost Continent." The New York Times, July 5, 1973, 18.
[26] Gerald R. Gems, *The Athletic Crusade: Sport and American Imperialism* (University of Nebraska Press: Lincoln, 2006), 68.
[27] Sharing Resources, A Community Learning Center, HawaiiHistory.org, Info Graik Inc., 2020.
[28] Robert M. Schoch. *Research Highlights: The Great Sphinx.* The Official Website of Robert M. Schoch, robertschoch.com/sphinx.html.
[29] Dwarka to Kurushetra. Dr. S. R. Rao. Journal of Marine Archaeology (1995-96).
Underwater Cultural Heritage. A.S Gaur and K. H Vora. Current Science Volume 86 No 9 May 2004.; Further Excavations of the Submerged City of

Dwarka. S. R. Rao. Recent Advances in Marine Archaeology
http://rafalreyzer.com/the-underwater-ruins-of-dwarka/

[30] Gil Haklay and Avi Gopher. 2020. Geometry and Architectural Planning at Göbekli Tepe, Turkey. Cambridge Archaeological Journal 30 (2): 343-357.

[31] Dan Rojas and Denise Rojas, Let's Melt Granite using a Fresnel Lens, Green Power Science.2016, GreenPowerScience.com.

[32] Larsen, Esper S. (1929). "The temperatures of magmas". American Mineralogist. 14: 81–94.

[33] Yu Zhou, Qiongqiong Tang, Shulei Zhang, and Dajun Zhao, Academic Editor: Hui Yao, *The Mechanical Properties of Granite under Ultrasonic Vibration*. Complex Condition Drilling Experiment Center, Jilin University, Changchun, China

[34] Richard Clem, Flame Speaker Science Fair Project, OneTubeRadio.com 2018, http://onetuberadio.com/2018/07/02/flame-speaker-science-fair-project/.

[35] K T. Ratcliffe, and Moody, R T.J. Wed. "The stratigraphy of the Taoudeni basin, west Africa". United States.

[36] Hui Chun Hing (2010). "Huangming zuxun and Zheng He's Voyages to the Western Oceans (A Summary)". Journal of Chinese Studies. 51: 85. Retrieved 15 January 2021. & Shan Henry Tsai

(2002). Perpetual Happiness: The Ming Emperor Yongle. University of Washington & "The Archaeological Researches into Zheng He's Treasure Ships". https://enacademic.com/dic.nsf/enwiki/20989. Retrieved 14 February 2021. & Richard Gunde. "Zheng He's Voyages of Discovery". UCLA Asia Institute. Archived from the original on 12 June 2008. Retrieved 28 January 2021.

[37] Ignatius Donnelly, *Discourse of "Critias,"* reprinted from "The Antediluvian World," (New York: Harper & Brothers), 1882.

[38] Randal Carlson, Sacred Geometry International, 2020 https://sacredgeometryinternational.com/randall-carlson/

[39] Brien Foester, Facebook page: https://www.facebook.com/Shipibospirit. Retrieved 10 February 2021

[40] Graham Hancock, *Graham Hancock: Biography*, 2020. https://grahamhancock.com/bio/

[41] *Charles C. Mann: About the Author*, Penguin-Random House, 2020. https://www.penguinrandomhouse.com/authors/60291/charles-c-mann/

[42] *Visiting Atlantis* https://visitingatlantis.com/

[43] *Visiting Atlantis Movie* https://visitingatlantis.com/Movie.html

[44] *Atlantipedia: AN A-Z Guide to the Search for Plato's Atlantis*,

https://atlantipedia.ie/samples/tag/george-s-alexander/

[45] Schoch, Robert M., *The Official Website of Robert M. Schoch*, https://www.robertschoch.com/index.html

[46] Zenter, Nick, Nick Zenter: I Teach Geology at Central Washington University, 2020. http://www.nickzentner.com

www.ingramcontent.com/pod-product-compliance
Lightning Source LLC
Chambersburg PA
CBHW060522100426
42743CB00009B/1405